Newham

Library
Service
01/08

= 4 MAR 2008	29 MAR 2009	
2 4 APR 2008	2 4 APR 2009	2 7 JUL 2011
2 9 JUN 2008	=7 DEC 2009	2 6 MAY 2012
1 5 JUL 2008	0 6 JUL 2010 7-1-10	
1 1 SEP 2008	- 3 OCT 2010	

24 hour automated
telephone renewal line
0115 929 3388

Or online at www.newham.gov.uk

**This book must be returned (or its issue renewed)
on or before the date stamped above**

D1471544

Prentice Hall LIFE

If life is what you make it, then making it better starts here.

What we learn today can change our lives tomorrow. It can change our goals or change our minds; open up new opportunities or simply inspire us to make a difference. That's why we have created a new breed of books that do more to help you make more of *your* life.

Whether you want more confidence or less stress, a new skill or a different perspective, we've designed *Prentice Hall Life* books to help you to make a change for the better. Together with our authors we share a commitment to bring you the brightest ideas and best ways to manage your life, work and wealth.

In these pages we hope you'll find the ideas you need for the life *you* want. Go on, help yourself.

It's what you make it

* * *

Financial Bliss

How to Grow Wealthy Together

Sarah Pennells

Pearson Education Limited
Edinburgh Gate
Harlow
Essex CM20 2JE
England

First published 2007

ISBN 978-0-273-71504-7

Commissioning editor: Emma Shackleton
Project editor and copy editor: Linda Dhondy
Designer: Kevin O'Connor
Cover design: Annette Peppis
Cover illustration: Nick Radford
Production controller: Neil Wilmot

Printed and bound by Henry Ling, UK

The Publisher's policy is to use paper manufactured from sustainable forests.

Contents

Acknowledgements

There are many people I want to thank for their willingness to share their knowledge and expertise, but there is one person who deserves a special mention and that is Denise Knowles, who is a family and relationship counsellor with Relate. I wanted this book to give financial advice within the context of a relationship and Denise gave me a valuable insight into the kinds of problems that money can cause and what couples can do to help themselves.

Many others have generously taken the time to help me, including Philip Rutter, a partner specializing in family law at Collyer Bristow, Karen Ritchie of independent financial advisers Financial Planning for Women, Ray Boulger of mortgage brokers John Charcol, Mary Webber of Advicenow, Kevin Carr of specialist brokers Lifesearch, Frances Walker of the Consumer Credit Counselling Service and several members of the Moneysupermarket.com team. In all cases, the expertise is theirs, any mistakes are mine.

I would also like to thank the team at Pearson Education; in particular Emma Shackleton for suggesting a book specifically aimed at couples and for her enthusiasm for the project, Paul East and Elie Ball, and Linda Dhondy for her expert editing.

I am also fortunate to have some very patient friends who read through various sections of the book for me. Lorraine McAvoy gamely checked the whole manuscript, while Dawn Goldsmith,

Martha Silcott, Caroline Watkin, Emma Daniel and Miriam Klein gave me useful feedback on specific chapters. I am grateful to you all. I would also like to mention Joe Adjei for his input and all those who provided quotes for the 'in their own words' sections. I appreciate their willingness to be open about a subject that many of us simply find too hard to talk about.

Sarah Pennells

Note: this book reflects the tax and legal situation as at November 2007, while all tax and benefit figures are for the tax year 2007–08.

Introduction: getting together

You've decided to get married or move in together. It's a big step and one that can be both incredibly exciting and a bit scary at the same time. (If, on the other hand, it's incredibly scary and only a bit exciting, check that you're not with the wrong person!)

So, why should you read a book about money? Surely you've got better things to do like plan the big day, decide whether you are going to rent or buy, or maybe just work out how your clothes are going to fit into your partner's flat without needing to build an extension. Well, one reason is that couples are more likely to argue about money than anything else. You'd think other things would be more likely to start rows, such as whether you spend enough time together, sex (not enough, too much, not the right kind), annoying habits, etc., but this is not the case.

Don't just take my word for it. There has been a lot of research over the years to back this up, but amongst the most authoritative is that carried out by the financial services regulator, the Financial Services Authority. It found that 75 per cent of couples find money the hardest subject to talk about. Around a third of couples were kept awake at night worrying about their money situation and around a quarter regularly argue when they try to talk about money.

1

And why does money lie at the root of all rows? It's probably because we don't talk constructively about it. While research shows that couples argue about money all too easily, talking about it is another matter. For whatever reason, money is still a bit of a taboo subject.

In some situations it can seem impolite to talk about money and with good reason. It's probably not recommended for a first date, unless you don't want a second one, but that doesn't mean you should *never* talk hard cash. And you should certainly make sure you do set aside time to have this conversation before you get financially entangled with your partner.

By that I mean before you take on big financial commitments, like a joint loan, a rental agreement or a mortgage. It doesn't mean you have to have a formal meeting and get out the flip charts, but you should get answers to any questions or concerns you may have and be prepared to answer your partner's.

That's easier said than done. You both have better things to talk about – and let's face it, spending an evening in together comparing bank statements is hardly likely to figure on your list of priorities.

If you can't or don't want to discuss money while you are just dating it's not such a big deal. As long as you don't have such different ideas about what you do with your cash that you argue about who spends what, you will probably be OK. However, it's all change when you decide to move in together, buy a home or get married. Any of these decisions takes your relationship to a different level and, whereas when you were going out it didn't matter if one of you was a spender and the other a saver, once you are married or own a home together it certainly does.

This book will help you deal with your financial differences and feel more confident about managing your money so that you can grow richer together. It will tell you how to recognize what the financial decisions you have already made mean for you as a couple and what legal rights you have once you get married or start living with your partner. But it will also give you a lot of practical advice on how to make the best decisions regarding your money, which in turn will help your relationship.

CHAPTER 1

Are you financially compatible?

There's one relationship in our lives that's very important to us, even though we probably don't acknowledge it. We may even be secretive about it. But how we manage it can be very revealing. I'm talking about our relationship with money.

Just as we have different ideas about what we want from a partner, so we have different ideas about money. In its simplest form, some of us think money is for spending while others reckon it's for saving for a rainy day.

Money, for many people, represents security or status. Someone who thinks their status is related to the amount of money they have may be keen to spend it – to show what they're worth – whereas if security is the main driving force they may prefer to save it. They know they feel anxious if they don't have 'enough' in the bank.

> If you understand what money means to you and are willing to learn what it means to your partner, you'll find it easier to deal with financial problems that may arise.

Opposites are supposed to attract, but if you have completely different ideas about money, you could have problems. Thankfully you and your partner don't have to have identical ideas about money for your relationship to work, but you do have to be able to recognize the differences and work out a way of dealing with them that suits you both.

> *In their own words:*
>
> *'My husband is generous to a fault, but he's not very good with money so when we got together he had quite a lot of debt, whereas I don't like to go overdrawn. But he told me about his debts early on which has meant we've been able to deal with it together.'*

Before you can work out what your partner is like, you need to know whether you're a money maestro or a money mess. So how would you describe yourself?

- **'I hate dealing with money and have only just managed to keep the bank and credit card companies at bay.'**

- **'I save a large slice of my earnings every month, know how much I have in my account and feel in control.'**

- **'I put off dealing with my money until I'm forced to, but can make some pretty good decisions if pushed.'**

OK, let's have a closer look at what you think money is for and how you feel about it. A key question is: do you feel in control of your money or does your money control you? Some of us have quite a guilty relationship with money. It's almost as though we don't really feel that we deserve it, so we don't treat it as a real part of our lives.

A few years ago I used to write 'money makeover' columns for a newspaper and was amazed at the number of people who held down demanding jobs, but found it hard to deal with their money. Many of them would say they had no debts, but actually owed several thousand pounds on credit cards. For some reason they didn't think of that as debt. Others just had no idea where their money went and, worse than that, they were embarrassed that they didn't feel in control. And that meant they ignored the problem.

In their own words:

'I've never found it that difficult to talk about money, but it's funny when you get married and suddenly you realize that everything is shared and there are no secrets. I was embarrassed to talk about my lack of organization with my money and the fact I owed money on my credit card.'

For some reason, being in a relationship doesn't seem to enhance our money management skills. Or certainly, it doesn't help us to communicate about cash. The Financial Services Authority's research showed that not only do 75 per cent of couples find money the hardest thing to talk about, but 30 per cent lie to their partners about how much they spend on credit cards and 1 in 20 split up over arguments about money.

Even in the closest of relationships, it's easy to believe that your partner is much more capable with money than you are or – conversely – that they haven't got a clue about cash. To get the best out of your money as a couple, you have to stop making assumptions and be honest, both with yourself and with your partner.

Quiz

This quiz is designed to give you some clues about your money behaviour. There are no right or wrong answers and no prize for finishing it in record time, so take your time over your answers.

1.   Your bank statement arrives. Do you:

a)   Shred it without opening it. Aren't banks always telling you to shred personal documents?

b)   Shove it in a drawer and promise to look at it later, but 'later' never arrives.

c)   Open it immediately. You know pretty much what it will say anyway.

2.   Your bank manager calls you. After you've recovered from the shock of being contacted by a real live bank manager (you thought they were extinct), do you:

a)   Immediately feel guilty. They must be about to give you a telling off.

b)   Think they must have the wrong number. You don't think there's any reason why they'd be in touch, but you're not completely sure.

c)   Realize that it must be in response to the call you made about savings accounts.

3.   You're at the shops and you spot a pair of shoes/iPod speakers that are nothing less than objects of beauty. Do you:

a)   Buy them. You can always cut down on something else next week.

b) Strike a deal with fate. If they're still in the shop next week, you'll buy them. You were obviously meant to have them. If they've gone, that's fate's way of saying no.

c) Work out whether you need them and whether you can really afford them. You know that this week's must-have can be next week's mistake.

4. You're at the same shop with the same lovely pair of shoes/iPod speakers. This time you've got no money. Do you:

a) Still buy them. That's what credit cards were invented for.

b) Raid your savings account – even though that's money for your holiday – and buy them. You're not buying on credit so what's the problem?

c) Wait until payday before you go near the shops again. If you still want the shoes/speakers and you know for sure you can afford them, you'll buy them.

5. You've had a long day at work and you've just realized there isn't much food in the fridge. You're also on a tight budget. Do you:

a) Ring a couple of mates and go out for a meal. Friends are more important than money anyway.

b) Buy a 'gourmet' ready-meal in the supermarket and a bottle of wine. After the day you've had you deserve a treat.

c) Spend a couple of pounds on ingredients and concoct something healthy that doesn't take long to make.

6. **You've got a pay rise. The extra money amounts to about £100 a month. Do you:**

a) Start spending the money in your mind. There are a few things you need right away.

b) Use the extra £100 to reduce your credit card debt. That pay rise has come just in time.

c) Spend a small amount on a treat (such as a lipstick or a DVD) and put the rest towards your savings or increasing your pension. You've managed without the money up until now.

7. **You've been saving some money. Is it:**

a) In a biscuit tin under your bed.

b) In an account that was paying a fairly good rate a couple of years ago. There's not much in it so there's little point in moving it around.

c) With a bank or building society that pays a top rate. You check the 'best buy' tables every few weeks to be sure.

8. **You've booked a holiday and it's only a few weeks away. Do you:**

a) Spend the next few weeks buying new outfits/ sunglasses/gadgets.

b) Decide you don't need anything, but then spend several hours at the airport buying books, sunglasses and duty-free gifts you won't use.

c) Work out what you can afford and set aside a treat budget. It's got to last you the whole holiday though.

9. **You are out for a meal with your partner. It's not a special occasion, just a chance to spend some time together. Your partner decides to order the wine and chooses an expensive £35 bottle. Do you:**

a) Happily drink it. You'll make sure they pick up the tab as well. When it's your turn to pay you'll simply choose something cheaper.

b) Spend the rest of the evening scowling. It's not that you're mean but £35 on wine for goodness sake!

c) Say something about it. You know that when money runs out your partner will expect you to pay.

10. **You receive a small inheritance of £5000. Do you:**

a) Spend it on anything that catches your eye. That's a lot of clothes and gadgets!

b) Spend it on the holiday of a lifetime. Life is for living.

c) Save it. That £5000 could buy you a new car in a few years' time, or just give you more 'rainy day' money.

What were your results?

Mainly 'a':
You probably have lots of fantastic qualities, but being good with money isn't one of them! You think money is for spending and when you run out, you're happy to spend the bank's and the credit card company's cash as well. The problem is that you will eventually have to settle your bills and that could be a hard day to face.

If you can be honest with yourself about your attitude to money, the next step is to take responsibility for your decisions. If you can't do that, you may struggle if you and your partner take on joint financial commitments.

Mainly 'b':

You make some good decisions, but then undo them by going on a spending spree. You have some money in your savings account (even though you don't know how much interest it's earning) and you don't automatically get your credit card out at every opportunity. But you're not completely confident and you don't always feel in control.

If you tackle your finances head-on so that you make better decisions, you'll be able to be clearer with your partner about what your own priorities are and where you'd like to be – in financial terms – in the future.

Mainly 'c':

You're definitely top of the class when it comes to your money. It's good that you're aware of the real cost of borrowing money and the fact that you have to check your savings accounts to get the best rates. You also understand the importance of budgeting and realize how easy it is to waste money on 'treats'. You know you're in charge of your money, which is how it should be.

But make sure that you don't fall into the trap of expecting your partner to match your own exacting standards, or becoming miserly in reaction to their spending.

What does it all mean for you as a couple?

The problem with doing these quizzes is that you can immediately see there's a 'goody two shoes' set of answers, an 'I'm lost in a sea of bills' set of answers and one that's somewhere in between. And a lot of us fit into the 'somewhere in between' section. But that doesn't really give the full picture. Even if both you and your partner fall into this category, you can have different ideas about what you want to do with your money. One of you may prefer to spend money on hobbies, the other on improving the house.

Differences like this don't have to be a problem, but they can be if you don't acknowledge your different ideas and understand that they may cause anxiety or resentment. For example, if you like to spend money on home improvements and your partner goes sailing or horse-riding (or something equally pricey), you may feel that your spending is 'better' than theirs. After all, yours benefits both of you, so of course it is!

So, does that make your partner selfish? Not necessarily. They may find that time spent on their hobby is one of the few occasions when they can relax. If it makes them feel better, that should bring its own benefit to the relationship.

In their own words:

'I bought a horse a few years before I met my partner. Now we've got a baby and at times money has been tight, but he's never suggested I get rid of my horse. He knows it's important to me.'

What happens if you have different ideas?

There are bound to be times when your partner does something you don't like. It will happen in relation to many areas of your life together and money is no different. If it's something you can accept – even if it's not your way of doing things – that's fine.

If you feel it's an issue that needs addressing, then you've got to be able to talk about it. If you can't talk about the 'difficult' subjects – like how you've run up debts and you've no idea how to pay them off – it's probably because you feel a bit embarrassed and guilty. According to counsellors who work for Relate (the relationship advice service), it could be a sign of insecurity, not necessarily about the relationship, but about how you feel about yourself.

With so many marriages and long-term relationships breaking down, there may be a niggling worry in one or both of your minds that yours may not last. If that's the case, shouldn't you be guarded with your money?

- Think about what money represents in your relationship. Is it about sharing and trust or do you think 'what's mine is mine and what's yours is ours'?

- Do you feel unnerved if your partner spends money when you wouldn't? Is it something you can talk about?

In their own words:

'I think money is the trickiest subject to discuss. Rob earned more than me and he felt that gave him the power to make all the decisions. It caused huge resentment.'

What happens if talking is too hard?

Relate counsellors continuously see couples who find talking too difficult, so if anyone should know how to help, they should. Here are some tips that have been passed on to clients over the years.

- If one of you is a spender and one is a saver, try to work out in advance what you'd do if the spender got into debt. It's much easier to talk about before the event than afterwards.

- Don't adopt an ostrich approach and hope problems will go away. They won't without help.

- Don't think your partner will change overnight.

Where do we go from here?

Take heart from the fact that you're even discussing money. That puts you ahead of many couples who only ever argue about it. But just as you learn to communicate with each other and compromise on a whole range of issues, so you can with money. Don't despair if it feels hard at this stage. If you follow the advice in this book, I guarantee that you'll find a way to increase the wealth you have while your relationship grows.

CHAPTER 2

What are you bringing to the relationship?

When you think about what you are bringing to the relationship, money probably isn't top of your list. How you feel about each other is number one. And that's down to what you have in common, what you expect from your relationship and how you spend time together. Isn't it? The answer is yes, yes and yes. But how you each feel about, earn, spend, save and use money is also important. And like it or not, the money or debts you've acquired are going to have an effect on your relationship.

Each of us has a financial footprint, a record of the financial decisions we've made:

- You may be a serial borrower, leaving a trail of credit cards and loans in your wake. You may have been caught out by how quickly your debts grew.

- You may be someone who's scrupulous about living within your means and been able to save even when cash was tight.

More likely there have been times when you've been a spender and others when you've been a saver. Whatever your financial history so far, it will not only affect what you can spend in the future, its impact could go beyond this.

The material impact is obvious. If one or both of you have spent your time as singletons racking up debts, it means you will begin your life together in debt. And that means you'll have less money to spend on yourselves as you pay back what you owe.

Buying something on credit can have long-term consequences on our finances, which we may be dealing with long after we've forgotten about or grown bored with whatever it was we bought in the first place.

It probably feels good at the time; you're able to buy something you want when you want it without worrying about what you have in the bank. For a lot of us, that's simply more enjoyable than saving up. You may even convince yourself that you'll pay off the bill in full when it arrives. But if you don't, and you end up paying interest, all you're doing is paying a high price (literally) for the purchases you've made.

> Think about the credit card and bank debt you may have, but don't beat yourself up about it. As long as you take the opportunity to look honestly at your situation and do something about it, you should end up on a better financial footing.

In their own words:

'I'm still paying off a very old credit card debt that has probably cost me more than £500 in fees and interest rates. It's such a lot to pay for a relatively small amount.'

Starting off in debt

These days the average student graduates with over £12,000 of debt. So it's impossible to leave university without being in debt. But the amount you owe may be much more than £12,000. Some debt is unavoidable, but you may have spent more than you needed to.

Whenever I've written articles about graduate debt and I've talked to students who owe many thousands of pounds, they tell me (virtually without exception) that they ended up borrowing more than they could afford because they felt ill-equipped to deal with the financial side of student life.

Even if you didn't carry on your education beyond school, you may have taken out a loan to buy your first car, or if budgeting isn't your strong point, you could have paid for your shoe/clothes/gadget weakness on your credit card. Research from CreditExpert. co.uk shows that a lot of us overspend because we make financial mistakes or through 'therapy spending'.

You probably recognize your own patterns and those of your partner:

- You've had a bad day at work. You buy a DVD or a few magazines on the way home. Either way you don't get much change from a tenner.

- A friend is going shopping and suggests you go too. You don't have any money but you know that buying a new outfit or computer game will cheer you up.

- You're going out on Friday night with some friends. You only planned to stay for a couple of drinks, but now they want to go to a club. After the week you've had, you feel you deserve a good night out.

It's not that spending money is bad, or even that spending money on treats is bad. Where it becomes a problem is if you don't stop to think how you're going to pay for it. And it can become an issue for you as a couple if you encourage each other's bad habits.

In their own words:

'When we first moved house we wanted to get it furnished and decorated as quickly as possible and didn't really consider how much it would cost in loans and credit cards. Spending got out of hand very quickly!'

Some would say the whole explosion of consumer credit is a sign that we're not getting the message that credit equals debt. Or that we're ignoring it. In the summer of 2007, according to the debt charity Credit Action, people in the UK owed over £1345 billion. Once you start adding that many zeros on the end of a figure, it's a bit too big for most brains to cope with. So, if you break those figures down:

- The average owed by every adult in the UK is £28,600 (including mortgages).

- The average personal borrowing (including credit cards, car loans and personal loans, but excluding mortgages) is £4550.

- However, not all adults have borrowings, so of those who do, the average personal debt is £10,200.

A nation of savers?

As the figures acknowledge, while we seem to be a nation of spenders and a country in love with credit, not everyone has debts. And even if we do, many of us also have some money put by. If either or both of you have been building up savings and/or investments before you got together, you'll be starting off several steps ahead.

Savings

The problem with using a term like savings is that it means different things to different people. A lot of us are reasonably good at saving for something like a holiday or stashing a bit of money in an account every month to pay for car repairs or to buy a new sofa. And some people have got saving down to a fine art and manage to squirrel away thousands of pounds simply by living well within their means and budgeting carefully.

If you fall into the latter category, you'll feel much more financially secure than someone who has only a few hundred pounds to their name. The mere fact that you've managed to save this kind of money speaks volumes about what your financial priorities are and the approach you take to managing your money.

> *In their own words:*
>
> *'When I got married I realized my husband was quite different to me. He'd always saved money whereas I hadn't always managed it – despite my best intentions.'*

She saves a little, he saves a lot

Here's an exercise for you: how much money do you have to your name at this very moment? And how much money does your partner have? Do you even know?

If you don't share your money, or if your relationship is in the early stages, you may not know. But the chances are that the one who's saved the most money is a man.

Figures from National Savings and Investments published in the summer of 2007 show that, on average, men aged 25–34 had £13,698 in savings, while women had over £6000 less at £7425. Research by the Fawcett Society, which campaigns for equality between men and women, found different levels of saving, but a similar trend. It found that women had £2000 put aside on average, whereas men had saved £3000. Women saved £75 a month; men saved £100.

So why do women save less than men? The fact that women generally earn less is a factor, but I don't think it's the only reason. A financial adviser I know spends a lot of her time advising women about their money and she's noticed, both in her professional capacity and from observing friends and family, that men are often more disciplined and focused when it comes to saving.

She's also noticed that when men and women earned the same, men would prioritize saving and would make sure they didn't dip into their money, whereas women would often raid their savings account if they 'needed' cash.

There are situations also where it can be impossible for women to save, such as if they stop work to bring up children, which adds to any savings imbalance that already exists.

In their own words:

*'I earned less than he did and the way he saw it was that money came out of **his** account for savings. Therefore he was saving and I wasn't. I showed him what I had coming in and going out, so that he could see that after all our bills, I didn't even have enough for a lipstick, let alone anything else.'*

The parental influence

Most of us get our basic grounding in money and how we perceive it from our parents. It doesn't necessarily mean you'll have the same approach as your mum and dad, but the chances are that you will be influenced by them – and probably more than you realize.

If your partner's parents had a different approach, it could explain why they don't share your views about money. So think about how often your parents talked to each other – and to you – about money when you were growing up. What are your memories about money when you were a child?

In their own words:

'Steve and I are very similar in that we both grew up in homes with relatively low incomes, so money was never taken for granted. We both had mothers who were very prudent and good at managing money. It means that we both value financial stability.'

Ask your partner what their experiences were. Was debt a dirty word or a guilty secret, or was it an everyday experience? See whether either of you recognizes any of these scenarios.

- If money was tight when you were growing up, you probably don't take it for granted now. You may find it hard to feel relaxed about your financial situation unless you have money in the bank.

- On the other hand your parents may have spent money as soon as it came in, even if cash was tight. That could mean you now feel you're better off living for today. Who knows what's around the corner?

Or perhaps your parents only ever argued about money and never discussed it calmly. You may therefore associate money with conflict and feel it's a force for bad rather than good.

Your first steps in the financial world

If you aren't sure how much of an influence your parents have been on the financial decisions you make today, you may get more of an idea if you look at those you've made along the way.

You need to get an overview: take stock, examine the decisions you've already made. You may each have a bank account and credit cards but have used them in very different ways. So, the end result would be that you would each bring a different financial footprint to your life together.

Bank accounts

You're unlikely to have got this far without a bank account, but while all current accounts do pretty much the same they're not identical. Whether you chose wisely when you opened your first account might have been down to luck rather than judgement. If you were a student you might have been tempted by the freebies. If you were working, you might have chosen a bank near your workplace or home, or one that offered telephone or internet banking.

What won't have been down to luck is how you've run your account since then. So, time to take a closer look. Do you:

Have money in your account at the end of the month?

Go into the red every month?

Even if you're both in credit or overdrawn by an identical amount each month, you could be in different financial shape. Some banks pay a healthy interest on credit balances, others a miserly rate. And if you go into the red, you'll pay hefty penalty charges if you don't tell the bank in advance. But some have reasonable rates on authorized overdrafts, so you could have chosen wisely.

Credit cards

You can't borrow money until you reach the age of 18. But it sometimes seems that as soon as you do, the floodgates open. You may be someone who hates the idea of credit cards and takes great delight in ceremoniously ripping up all the offers that come through your letterbox. But your partner may collect credit cards rather like kids collect football stickers, desperate to get the 'full set'.

Look at how you each use your cards and who's in control here. Are you using your cards so you can benefit from interest-free credit or because without them you don't have enough money to live on?

Why credit cards can be good

By paying off your credit card every month you will each have been building up your credit record which means lenders are more likely to see you as a good risk, and that will help you get access to loans at competitive interest rates.

...and why they can be bad

If, however, one or both of you are managing to pay off only the minimum amount every month or have missed payments, you may be seen as a riskier prospect by financial companies and you could end up being charged higher interest if you borrow money.

More importantly, interest on credit card debts can mount up worryingly fast. Most cards ask you to pay a minimum of 3 per cent of your bill every month, although some let you pay as little as 2 per cent.

The price comparison web site uSwitch (www.uswitch.com) calculated that if someone with the average credit card debt of £1812 paid back only 2 per cent a month, it would be over 29 years before they were debt free. The total they'd have paid back would be £2858, so they'd have given the credit card company £1000 for the privilege of borrowing £1800.

Store cards

Here's a very simple message: store cards are a really bad idea. So if you or your partner has one, or even worse, a handful of store cards, you're probably not the best money managers.

There is one exception – if you manage to play the companies at their own game. So if you take one out to get the 'account opener's discount' (which is typically 10–15 per cent off your first purchase) and clear the bill in full when it arrives, you won't have paid any interest. Now we've got the exception out of the way, why are store cards such a bad idea? Simple: because the interest rates can be sky-high.

Hardly surprising then that it's hard to visit a department store or fashion retailer without being stalked by a sales assistant brandishing an application form. These cards are a gold mine for the companies providing them.

In their own words:

'Years ago I had a store card which I didn't pay off in full. It was so silly because I ended up paying a lot in interest for something that wasn't very expensive in the first place. I've never done it since.'

Loans

In some ways it's not the amount you may have borrowed in loans, it's what you've borrowed it for that says the most about you both. In the current climate, we're being given very mixed messages about debt, but not all debt is bad. You can't get a degree or buy a house without taking on debt and life without some debt is virtually impossible. Have you taken out loans to finance your way through university or to buy a car? Or do you have a loan because you're using it to pay off credit card debts or an overdraft?

So, even if you each have a loan, that doesn't necessarily mean you can't manage your money. And if you have managed to secure a competitive interest rate that's definitely a good sign. As long as you make all the repayments on time, you will improve your credit rating as lenders start to build up a picture of how you handle credit.

But if you or your partner has taken on a loan that's at an uncompetitive interest rate, or one that you are struggling to afford, you could be hundreds – or even thousands – of pounds worse off.

Tell-tale signs of a bad deal

- *Uncompetitive interest rate*: While you can get loans at between 0.5 per cent and 3 per cent above the Bank of England base rate, you can also pay a lot more. A quick search on the internet showed some high street banks charging significantly more – sometimes up to 9 per cent above the base rate.

- *Payment protection insurance (PPI)*: Banks and credit card companies love to sell us PPI when we take out a loan or credit card. The reason is simple: it makes them so much

money. Paying these premiums is often little better than tearing up £10 notes, because many of the policies have so many catches that they rarely pay out.

In Chapter 4 I'll be looking in detail at how you can switch to a better interest rate if you're paying too much for your loan, how to switch to a cheaper PPI policy, and what to do if you think you were mis-sold the policy in the first place.

Mortgages

You may not start the relationship with a mortgage in your own right, although it's certainly not out of the question. You may have managed to get on the property ladder under your own steam or teamed up with friends or parents to buy.

Advantages of a home loan of your own

If you do have a mortgage on your own flat then in some ways you're one step ahead if and when you come to buy somewhere with your partner. You'll have had the chance to build up some equity (unless property prices have fallen). You may also have an idea about the kind of mortgage you'd like in the future.

...and the disadvantages

There's only really one downside to having a mortgage at this stage and that is if it's not flexible enough to cope with any changes in your lifestyle – namely, if you want to buy somewhere with your partner and you're locked into an uncompetitive rate, or to a lender that isn't very flexible.

Money in the bank

If you've got into the savings habit at an early age, you're doing well. You may have started saving without even realizing it, if your parents or grandparents opened an account for you when you were young. The question is, have you grown out of the savings habit? Research by AXA (the insurance company) found that 33 per cent of UK adults had saved nothing at all.

If you think about how your earnings increase throughout your working life, it should follow that the older you are, the more you are able to save. And that's what AXA found.

- **Young adults aged 16–24 had saved £631 on average.**

- **Adults aged 25–34 had set aside £1001 on average.**

- **Adults aged 55–64 had saved the most: £1227 each.**

Interestingly the company found a direct link between the amount of time people spend sorting out their finances and how much they save. So if you or your partner don't open your bank statements, or just skim over them to make sure they're not a complete work of fiction, you're far less likely to put money aside every month than someone who checks these and is aware of other financial deals.

Dig out some of your bank statements – preferably for the last year. Look at how much you've set aside in savings and what you spend on your financial weakness (it may be clothes, gadgets or going out). You probably know instantly what your weakness is, but I bet you don't know how much it's costing you.

Now compare the two. Which is greater? If you're saving *a lot* more than you're spending on your financial weakness, you're at least getting your priorities right. How does your partner compare?

In their own words:

'Adam did not save at all, whereas I always tried to. I've always felt I've wanted to have a comfort zone of money I could dip into if I needed it.'

Some advice

I've talked about why it's such a good idea to have savings, but there's one situation where it doesn't make sense and that's if you've built up debts. Many of us like the idea of keeping our cash in separate pots, but if you're paying anything between 6 per cent and 30 per cent in interest on your debts (depending on the kind of debt you have) and earning between only 0.1 per cent and 8 per cent on your savings .... well, you do the maths.

Investments

Most people don't manage to start serious investing until their thirties (and sometimes later), so don't worry too much if you've not had the chance to build up your investments. But you may have managed to put aside some money into an ISA (Individual Savings Account) or similar product, or your parents or grandparents may have taken out an investment plan for you.

The fact that one or both of you has some money invested is a good sign in itself, because it means you're comfortable thinking about the longer term with regard to your money. And that's the key to successful investing.

Pension

A lot of us 'don't trust' pensions, but the fact is most people aren't saving anything like enough for their retirement. The Association of British Insurers puts the savings gap at between £27 billion and £31 billion a year, which seems both scary and rather meaningless at the same time. I'll talk more about pensions in Chapter 6. But if you are investing for your retirement, it's a positive step and if you're not then what are you going to live on when you stop work?

What does my financial footprint look like?

You've probably read through the last few pages and been able to tick off at least three or four different financial commitments, whether it's a bank account, credit card or savings account. What does it add up to? More importantly, what impact might your financial footprint have on your relationship or vice versa?

One way that your financial footprint could affect your relationship relates to your credit status. The amount of money you've borrowed over the years and – more importantly – how you've paid it back has a measurable impact on how banks, credit card companies and even mail order companies and mobile phone providers view you.

If you're a good credit risk, you'll be able to get the best deals – to borrow money at the lowest rates and to take your pick of credit cards and mortgages. If you're seen as a bad risk you may find it hard to get credit – or at the very least you'll have to pay more for it.

You're on file

You won't find out what the banks and building societies think of you unless you ask for a copy of your credit reference file. It is a record of the loans and credit agreements you've taken out, how much you owe and how much you've repaid.

To get the full picture, you should make sure you get a copy of your file from at least two of the three credit reference agencies, Equifax, Experian and Call Credit. It's worth doing because it could alert you or your partner to potential problems. If you know there's an issue, you may be able to do something about it in good time. By law you're allowed to receive a copy of your file for £2.

> *In their own words:*
>
> *'I sent away for a copy of my credit reference file and it had details of someone else's address on it – someone I don't know. It took several weeks and quite a few phone calls to get it sorted.'*

According to the consumer organization Which? 70 per cent of people have never checked their file while one in five of those who did check found a mistake. Some people don't access their file because they don't realize how powerful the information is that's stored on it. Others don't want to see their file because they're worried about what they may find out.

I can understand why you might not want to see in black and white what you already suspect, but the truth is whether you see your credit file or not, plenty of others will. Whenever you take out a credit agreement, you give permission for information about how you pay back the money to be shared. That information is already out there and available for hundreds of lenders to see any day of the week, so the least you can do is check it's accurate.

What does a credit reference file contain?

Your file carries information about where you live at the moment and any addresses you've lived at over the past six years. It will include 'publicly available information' such as whether you are on the Electoral Roll and will also list any County Court Judgments (CCJs) that are registered against you if you live in England and Wales and any Decrees issued against you in Scotland. In addition, your file will state whether you have been declared bankrupt or entered into an individual voluntary arrangement (IVA) or whether you've had a sequestration against you if you live in Scotland. The most important part is a record of all your credit agreements, how much you owe and how you've repaid them.

CCJs and Scottish Decrees

A CCJ or Decree is simply a record of the fact that someone took you to the local county court or sheriff's court to try to get you to pay back money you owed. It could have been an individual (such as a builder or plumber) or a company (such as an energy supplier or a bank).

The reason that CCJs and Decrees are so serious is that they can mess up your credit record for six years. But if you can pay off the CCJ or Decree within a month of it being registered against you by the court , then you can ask the court to cancel and remove it from your records. It will also be removed from your credit file, so no damage will have been done to your credit status. But it's probably worth getting hold of a copy of your file anyway to make sure it's been done.

If you leave it longer than a month before you pay off the debt the CCJ or Decree will remain on your file, but if you send proof of payment to the court, it will be marked as 'satisfied' on your credit reference file. That's better than an unpaid CCJ or Decree, but it will still remain on file for six years.

How to get your file

You can ask for a hard copy of your file by paying £2 but you can also get it for free from all three agencies by signing up for a 30-day trial for their credit alert services. You'll need to give credit card details, so don't forget to cancel or you'll end up being charged after 30 days.

Contact details

Equifax:
Credit File Advice Centre,
PO Box 1140, Bradford, BD1 5US
Phone: 0870 0100 583
Web site: www.equifax.co.uk

Experian:
Consumer Help Service,
PO Box 8000, Nottingham, NG80 7WF
Phone: 0870 241 6212
Web site: www.experian.co.uk

Call Credit:
Consumer Services Team,
PO Box 491, Leeds, LS3 1WZ
Phone: 0870 0601414
Web site: www.callcredit.co.uk

Misleading information

If you got behind with your payments, it will be recorded on file, but there will be no explanation of the reasons why. However, you can add a 200-word explanation (called a notice of correction) of how you came to be in debt or behind with payments. It may be that you lost your job, or moved house and didn't get the final demands, etc. Make sure you send the notice of correction to all three agencies, so that all lenders and credit suppliers will see it.

The notice of correction can also be a useful way of explaining why you're not on the Electoral Roll (for example, if you've recently moved) or why you've moved address so many times (for example, if you're in the armed forces).

Correcting a mistake

If you see something on your file that is incorrect, you can have it put right. Tell the credit reference agency what you think is wrong and they'll contact the lender on your behalf (which is called 'raising a dispute'). They don't have to sort out the problem instantly, but they do have to get back to you within 28 days and give you a progress report. In the meantime, any information that you have queried is marked as disputed and a prospective lender is not allowed to rely on it.

Help, I'm being ignored!

If you feel you're getting nowhere with your complaint, you have two possible courses of action. You can complain to the Financial Ombudsman Service (www.financial-ombudsman.org.uk), which is a free complaints service that covers the whole of the financial services industry, or the Information Commissioner (www.ico.gov.uk). The Information Commissioner oversees the way companies keep and exchange data about us.

The next steps

Wherever you are now, you – and your money – could be in a better position in the future. All you need to do is face up to your situation together and put some sound financial plans in place.

The key is to support each other so you can both learn and give encouragement about making money choices. The quicker you can pay off your debts and get a cushion of savings behind you, the more comfortable and confident you will feel. But don't worry if you have to start with small steps. It's the direction you travel in that's important, not necessarily the speed at which you set off.

CHAPTER 3

You and the law

According to the Frank Sinatra song, 'love and marriage go together like a horse and carriage', and marriage is still something that a lot of us say we want. In a *Sunday Telegraph* poll (carried out by ICM in July 2007 and published later in the same month), 80 per cent of people questioned said that marriage was personally important to them. That may be so, but the fact is that many marriages do not survive and some people only realize the legal implications of marriage when they split up.

Meanwhile the number of couples choosing to live together has been increasing steadily for some time and it's estimated that the figure now stands at around 2 million. The problem is that the law has not kept up with this trend, as many couples discover when things go wrong. Cohabiting couples in England, Wales and Northern Ireland have very few rights, and although changes to the law mean couples are better protected in Scotland, they don't have the same rights as married couples.

One area where there has been significant change in the law is the creation of civil partnerships, which gives same-sex couples the same financial rights as married couples.

Whether you decide to get married, enter into a civil partnership or live together is down to you. What this chapter will do is explain what your legal rights and responsibilities are so that, whatever you do, you will know where you stand financially and legally.

For better, for worse

Marriage has become a political issue over the years with endless debates about whether successive governments are doing enough to encourage it. And that debate is likely to continue if the number of couples getting married carries on falling. Figures from the Office of National Statistics show that in 2005 (the latest year for which there is accurate data), the number of couples tying the knot fell by 10 per cent to 245,000.

Meanwhile the Law Commission has published a preliminary report on whether it's time to give cohabiting couples better rights in law. It certainly doesn't mean that the law will change – that decision is down to the government – but it may be a recognition that either the law *should* change or people who live together need to be given more information about their rights.

> There is one situation where it doesn't matter whether you are married, in a civil partnership or living together, and that's in relation to your children. If you have children, you're both responsible for supporting them financially.

For richer, for poorer

If you take a long, hard look at what you get by way of financial rights from being married, most of them don't apply until the point of divorce or death. It's probably not the most reassuring thought if you're contemplating walking up the aisle, but if we're talking cash, there are only limited financial benefits to being Mr & Mrs as opposed to Mr & Ms. However, these benefits can make a difference to a couple's finances, which is one reason why the creation of civil partnerships was seen as so important by many gay and lesbian couples.

You don't have to say 'I do' to inheritance tax

Inheritance tax (IHT) used to be something that only the wealthiest people paid. However, decades of soaring house prices have changed all that. In the current tax year (2007/08), you have to pay IHT (or rather, the person sorting out your affairs has to pay it out of your 'estate') if the property and investments, etc. that you leave add up to more than £300,000, which is the IHT threshold. That's something of an over-simplification, because a whole industry has grown up around inventive ways of avoiding IHT. But you don't need to take out a clever policy; one easy way to beat it is to get married or enter into a civil partnership.

If you're married or in a civil partnership, you can leave all your worldly goods to your spouse or civil partner when you die and your estate won't have to pay a penny in IHT. And when they die, they can leave up to twice the IHT threshold (2 x £300,000) without there being tax to pay.

> *In their own words:*
> *'We've lived together for years but now we've got children, we've begun to worry about IHT and wonder whether it's worth getting married.'*

Other tax benefits

The good news, if you're married or in a civil partnership, is that you can also give anything you want to your spouse or civil partner and they won't have to pay capital gains tax (CGT) on it – no matter how valuable it is. It means you can give away assets to minimize your tax bill.

Capital gains tax is a tax you pay on the profit you make when you sell assets such as share investments or a second property. You don't have to pay CGT on every penny of profit as you're given an annual allowance (£9200 in 2007/08). You can reduce your CGT bill in two ways: by giving away assets or by owning them jointly so you use up two lots of your annual allowance.

> Bear in mind that if you give away something to your spouse or civil partner, you can't ask for it back. You may save tax but if you split up you could end up much worse off.

Your pension

If you are married or in a civil partnership, you may also get some benefits relating to both state and work pensions.

- *State pension*: **In order to get the full state pension, you must have made sufficient National Insurance contributions (NICs). At the moment a wife who hasn't done so can claim a state pension worth 60 per cent of her husband's pension based on his NICs. It doesn't work the other way around currently, although change is on the way and from 2010 both husbands and civil partners will be able to claim a state pension this way.**

- *Company or occupational pension schemes*: **Most pension schemes will pay a percentage of the pension you have built up to your spouse or civil partner when you die.**

Anyone who is dependent on you financially (such as a child) would also be able to claim this pension. However, not all schemes will let you nominate a partner you live with as a dependant. It will be down to the pension scheme trustees (those who run the scheme for the company and its employees) and the pension scheme's own rules.

Rights at divorce or dissolution

In Chapter 10 the practicalities of what you can do if you are contemplating divorce or the breakup of a civil partnership are covered, but it's worth knowing what rights you have if you decide you can't stay together.

The UK has been described as the 'divorce capital of the world' and if you've read the papers recently, you'll know that some seriously wealthy people (normally, but not exclusively, husbands) have ended up handing over large sums of their money to their ex-spouses. However, divorce doesn't actually mean 'big payouts', or that one party will automatically walk away with a large chunk of the joint wealth.

What marriage (and a civil partnership) does, though, is put in place some safeguards so that a spouse or civil partner can't walk away from their financial obligations on divorce. In very general terms the starting point for splitting the assets is a 50:50 split of money and property that were either bought or built up during the marriage. However, the courts will take all kinds of factors into account, so the final settlement may not be an equal division at all.

In Scotland, the situation relating to assets and property is different and any property that a married couple has acquired during the marriage or for the marriage is divided equally.

Property in death

If you're married or in a civil partnership your spouse or civil partner will automatically inherit *some* of the money and/or property you leave, even if you haven't made a will.

In basic terms, if you live in England or Wales and have children your spouse or civil partner can inherit the first £125,000 worth of money and property plus what is called a 'life interest' in half the rest. In Northern Ireland the 'life interest' element depends on the number of children. If there are no children, the spouse or civil partner would receive the first £200,000 plus half the rest.

In Scotland the rules are different. A spouse or civil partner has 'prior rights', which means they have a right to the house worth up to £300,000. If the house is worth more, the situation can become complex. If you own your home jointly *in some circumstances* it can automatically pass to the surviving spouse or partner when the other dies. There are more details about this in Chapter 5.

Why living together is not marriage by another name

If you live with your partner but aren't married, you don't have much by the way of legal rights. In fact, I could probably write them on a postage stamp and still have room left over.

The only exception to this is in Scotland, where couples who live together have been given certain rights if they were living together on 4 May 2006 or have started living together since then, which is when the Family Law (Scotland) Act came into force.

The Act says that when a couple live together, some things they've acquired during that period are presumed to belong to them both. The Act also allows cohabitants to make a claim against their former partner if the relationship breaks down or if the former partner dies without leaving a will.

If one partner dies without a will in Scotland, the surviving partner can go to court to make a claim on their estate. However, there are no guarantees about how much they will receive as this will depend on who else has a claim on the estate and the circumstances of the surviving partner (for example, if they received any other money on their partner's death, say from a pension). A former partner cannot receive more than they would have had they been married to the deceased.

What the Law Commission is proposing

The idea is not that couples who live together have the same rights as those who get married but that one partner would be able to go to court to seek a share of the property or a lump sum if the couple split up and they were left seriously out of pocket. Not all live-in relationships would qualify, but some would. These include:

- couples who have lived together for a 'qualifying' length of time, which would probably be at least two years *and*

- where one partner has made a significant contribution to the relationship, whether it's financial – such as paying towards the mortgage on their partner's house – or a practical contribution – say where they've given up work to look after the children

- couples who live together and have a child together (in which case the qualifying period wouldn't apply).

Under the proposals, cohabiting couples would also have more rights if one partner died without making a will. It wouldn't mean the surviving partner would *automatically* inherit, as is the case with married couples, but it would be easier to go to court.

Just to reiterate the point, the government hasn't said it wants to see a change in the law, so *if* there's a change, it could be several (or many) years off.

Current rights for cohabiting couples

The situation as it stands at the moment is pretty complicated, made worse by the fact that it's not easy to find information on what rights you might have. However, there is a really good web site at www.advicenow.org.uk. This independent, legal advice web site contains a large information section on cohabitation. There are agreements to download and user-friendly guides to what happens to your children, money and property if one of you dies or you split up.

For many couples, the biggest purchase they make is their home. But what happens to it if the relationship breaks down is by no means clear.

- *If the home is owned in one person's name*: If you break up and the home you've been sharing is in one person's name, even if you both paid towards it, the person whose name is not on the deeds could have no claim on the property – or be forced to go to court to prove the financial contribution they made.

- *If you both paid towards the property*: If, for example, you helped your partner buy their property at the time they bought it (perhaps by providing a deposit), you should get a share of the property's value based on your contribution. If your partner is unwilling to pay up, you have to be prepared to go to court. Similarly if one partner paid towards the mortgage or for major works to the home, such as an extension, they might be able to get a share of the property, but again they would have to be prepared to go to court. It helps if there is evidence of the bills having been paid (for example, bank statements, receipts or cheque-book stubs).

Taking your case to court could involve several thousand pounds in legal fees and would undoubtedly be an emotionally draining experience. Even if you're successful in court, you may then have to ask the court to make an order that the house should be sold to get your share paid.

If your home is owned jointly

You may think that if you both own your home, it should all be fairly straightforward. Well, yes and no. It is straightforward in that both of you will have rights to *some* of the proceeds of the sale of the property, but how the property is split will come down to the legal arrangement you have in place.

I'll go through the options in detail in the section on buying a home together but, in broad terms, you can own a property jointly as 'joint tenants' or 'tenants in common'.

In their own words:

'My partner earns quite a lot and I'm not working as I'm bringing up our son, so he's paid far more towards the house. I worry that if we split up, I might get very little.'

42

Joint tenants

If you buy your house or flat as joint tenants, it means you own it *equally* – no matter how much each of you actually pays towards the mortgage, etc. If you were to split up, the proceeds of the sale would generally be split 50:50 between you. You would have to convince the court that you'd paid a lot more towards the house than your partner to get a greater share.

Tenants in common

It's a different matter if you buy as tenants in common. What this enables you to do is to set out, in a legal document, how much of the property each of you owns. So, if one of you earns less than the other and, for example, is contributing a third of the deposit and monthly mortgage payments, you could decide that you will split the way you own the property as one third:two thirds. As long as you have a formal document called a 'declaration of trust' drawn up to say who owns what, it would be divided on the same basis if you were to split up.

However, if you don't have a declaration of trust in place, the presumption will be that you own it 50:50. A court case that went all the way to the House of Lords in 2007 reiterated this. It centred on a couple – Barry Stack and Dehra Dowden – who had lived together for 20 years. They had bought a house in joint names, but hadn't specified how the ownership should be divided.

Although in their case the Law Lords decided that the split should be 65:35 in favour of Ms Dowden because she'd provided the deposit from the proceeds of the sale of her previous property (which was registered in her name only), they said it was an unusual case. In most cases, if an agreement hadn't been drawn up, the presumption would be that the property would be owned 50:50.

> Just because you buy as tenants in common does not mean you automatically own the property on an unequal basis. If you don't state how you want the property to be owned through a declaration of trust, it will be assumed that you own it on a 50:50 basis.

Living together in rented property

You might think that if you don't own your property, but rent it instead, the situation would be much simpler. Unfortunately, because there are several different kinds of rental agreement, that's not necessarily the case.

You may be renting a flat or house with your partner, but have the rental agreement in your name, in their name or in joint names, and this will affect your rights should you split up.

A living together agreement

It's not a pre-nup, more like a pre-cohab and it's the easiest way to avoid the expense and stress of going to court. Put simply, it's a written agreement about what would happen to your property and possessions should you split up. It's something that few couples do, but I think these agreements are a good idea.

Having such an agreement doesn't show you don't expect the relationship to last, or that you don't trust your partner. It just means that if you do split up, you're less likely to have a battle over who gets what. Advicenow (an independent service) has a comprehensive and easy-to-follow living together agreement that can be downloaded from http://www.advicenow.org.uk/fileLibrary/pdf/Living_Together_Agreements.pdf

In their own words:

'I wish we'd had an agreement drawn up when we bought our house together. It would seem odd to do it now – like I was expecting us to split up.'

Pre-nuptial agreements

The rise in the number of 'big money' divorces has invariably sparked greater interest in pre-nuptial agreements. Sometimes it seems like everyone either has one, is thinking about having one or regrets the fact they haven't. But the truth is that pre-nuptial agreements are still pretty rare and until a few years ago were strictly the preserve of the seriously wealthy. A divorce case in 2000 that changed the way courts divided assets prompted more people to think about making one.

Where pre-nups are often used is to set out in a contract that each partner is allowed to keep any assets they've built up before the marriage. An increasing number of younger people who've made money on their first property are using pre-nups to ring-fence that equity.

Another situation where pre-nups are becoming more common is where one partner has inherited some money or is likely to inherit in the near future. In that case, it is often the donor who wants the pre-nuptial agreement drawn up, not necessarily the bride or groom. And more people are marrying for a second or even third time and they may want to limit the impact of a financial settlement.

> Pre-nups are more common in America, where they are also much more wide-ranging. There, a pre-nup can be used effectively to 'regulate' many aspects of the relationship within a marriage (such as whether someone puts on weight or is unfaithful, etc.).

Part of the reason why they're not more popular in the UK (apart from the fact that some couples think it's unromantic, cynical even, to ask the love of your life to promise not to become a money-grabbing schemer in the event of a divorce!) is that they inhabit a rather strange legal no-man's land.

At the moment, divorce courts in England, Wales and Northern Ireland can take notice of pre-nuptial agreements, but they are not legally binding. That means they are worth more than the paper they're written on, but not necessarily much more.

It's a different situation in Scotland, where both pre- and post-nups are now common and thought to be legally enforceable. Their legal status can be influenced by some factors, such as where and how the pre-nup is drawn up and where the divorce takes place.

So, when should you think about making a pre-nuptial agreement and what can you do to increase your chances of it standing up in court? The key is to make sure there's no sign of coercion. The way the courts see it, the nearer the wedding day, the more likely you are to sign something even if you're not entirely comfortable with it.

- Ideally, pre-nuptial agreements should be drawn up and signed at least 21 days before the wedding.

- You each have to provide a summary of your financial situation.

- Both of you must take independent legal advice. This is obviously designed to show that you've been given unbiased information about the likely consequences of signing the pre-nup.

The pre-nup must not be 'manifestly unfair' to one party, for example an agreement that states each party keeps their own assets, where one is on a very low salary and the other earns a small fortune.

What's in a pre-nup?

A straightforward pre-nup will either state that assets owned or built up before the marriage will be kept separate and won't form part of any financial settlement in the event of a divorce, or it will state that assets (including gifts or inheritances given to either party) will be divided 50:50 in the event of a divorce.

One problem with pre-nups is that they can quickly become dated. What seemed like a fair settlement at the start of a marriage may not seem fair after 10 or 20 years. So, a good pre-nuptial agreement will have a clause saying that it should be reviewed after 5–10 years and/or after the birth or adoption of a child. Some pre-nups can be quite sophisticated and pre-empt this with a built-in review.

Post-nups

You might wonder why someone would want to sign up to an agreement limiting what they may get in the event of a divorce, once they're already married, but while post-nuptial agreements are far less common than pre-nups, their numbers are also beginning to increase. The principle is similar to the pre-nup, but they're mainly used to protect an inheritance rather than assets that have been built up by one party. So a parent who was giving their son or daughter some money might insist on a post-nup.

What your rights mean for you

Most of us don't think about the legal rights we have in our everyday lives and I'm not suggesting that you should become legal experts before you contemplate a closer step in your relationship, but it's important that you know the financial benefits to marriage or being in a civil partnership.

If you're planning to live together, understanding how limited your rights will be should mean you can put in place some safeguards in case the relationship does fail.

CHAPTER 4

The road to financial bliss

If you want your finances to develop and grow alongside your relationship, you have to give them a helping hand. And the first step on the road to financial bliss is to work out where your money goes now. If you don't know the answer, you need to find out. One of the best ways to do this is to keep a money or spending diary.

It may not sound like fun, but keeping a diary will help you see whether or not you're making the best use of your cash. Write down what you spend, what you spend it on and when you spend it. Don't underestimate how good you'll feel once you have a clearer idea of what you're spending your money on. If you've never kept a spending diary before, you probably won't think it will make much of a difference – but believe me, it will.

I know because I kept one for the first time a number of years ago when I always seemed to run out of money before the end of the month. A friend of mine who was a financial adviser suggested I write down what I was spending. I thought it was a slightly sad thing to do, but decided to give it a go. Within a week or two it was obvious that I was spending far more on some things than I realized. It was a real revelation (and something of a shock). And once I saw it in black and white, it was much easier to cut back.

Unless you already keep a spreadsheet of all your spending, or are confident you don't waste your cash, it's worth keeping a diary. If you need any more convincing, think about this:

- Are you happy with your current relationship with money? Or do you have moments when you worry about your finances?

- How would you feel if you knew you had enough money in the bank to comfortably last you until the end of the week or month and had some savings so you could pay for your next holiday?

Changing your habits is hard. If you've happily muddled along until now it may feel easier to carry on. But, if you're spending more than you're earning, it's not a very sustainable way to live. If something in your life changes (you lose your job, fall ill or you or your partner become pregnant) you could find that your rather precarious arrangements come crashing down.

> Ideally, you should keep a diary for at least three months, so you can record spending on things like birthday and Christmas presents, car insurance, etc., but don't worry about that when you begin. If it makes it easier, tell yourself you'll only keep it for a week. It really doesn't matter how you manage to 'bribe' yourself to get started – just start.

What your spending diary shows

Don't view the task as one that you've got to pass or fail. Many of us spend money on things we shouldn't/can't afford/wish we hadn't. But by keeping a diary, what's likely to happen is that as soon as you start writing everything down, you'll spend less. It's an understandable reaction: it may be the first time you've actually added up what you spend every day.

> *In their own words:*
>
> *'We never know how much we spend – either individually or as a couple. I worry about it but I'm also scared about doing anything about it. In some ways ignorance is bliss.'*

If the results of your spending diary come as a bit of a shock, don't worry. The worst thing to do is to think that your spending habits are beyond salvation. Believe me, they're not. If you're willing to make some changes, you can really turn around what might seem like quite a bad financial situation into a much healthier one.

The next step

Once you know where you are spending your money now, the next step is to work out what you can actually afford and what you should be spending your money on. By that, I mean drawing up a budget.

Like keeping a spending diary, drawing up a budget isn't exciting, sexy or glamorous, but then neither is arguing about credit card bills or being too frightened to open your bank statement. Just keep in mind the thought that once you've done it, you'll be in a better position in relation to your money than before you started.

What's in a budget?

Unlike your spending diary, where you write down absolutely everything you spend, a budget breaks down what you have coming in and where your money goes. You want the process of drawing up a budget to be as easy as possible, so use a software program or a budget template like the one opposite.

Sample budget

The table opposite is based on one that you can find on the Financial Services Authority's web site (www.moneymadeclear.fsa. gov.uk), but there are plenty of others on the internet.

You may have to tailor the template to your specific circumstances. The key is to ensure you include all your spending. That way you can make any necessary cuts.

Big debts, small income

If you're in serious trouble (i.e. you're being threatened by debt collectors or bailiffs or you just know you can't go on as you are), you should get some help. But you don't *have* to be in serious trouble to do that, so don't be afraid to ask. There are several places you can go for free advice, so there's no need to pay someone to sort out your debts.

Don't worry about what the debt advisers may think about the state of your finances. Whatever you tell them, you can guarantee they'll have heard it all before. Debt advisers are not there to judge you, but to help.

Debt advice services I'd recommend include Citizens Advice (www.citizensadvice.org.uk), which has bureaux in many towns and cities. All give debt help and some have specialist money advisers. The Consumer Credit Counselling Service (CCCS) is another

Money coming in	How much (£)?
NET PAY (after tax has been taken off)	....
OVERTIME/BONUS OR COMMISSION (don't use the example of your best month, try to average it out)	....
STATE BENEFITS	....
INTEREST FROM SAVINGS	....
CHILD MAINTENANCE	....
RENTAL INCOME	....
SHARE DIVIDENDS	....

Money going out	How much (£)?
MONTHLY BILLS/SPENDING – YOUR HOUSE	
MORTGAGE / RENT	....
COUNCIL TAX	....
GAS	....
ELECTRICITY	....
LANDLINE PHONE/MOBILE/INTERNET	....
TV LICENCE/SATELLITE	....
WATER	....
OTHER	....
FINANCIAL PRODUCTS	
CREDIT CARD(S)	....
STORE CARD(S)	....
BANK LOAN	....
PENSION CONTRIBUTION	....
MONEY PAID INTO SAVINGS ACCOUNT(S)	....
MONEY PAID INTO INVESTMENT(S)	....
LIFE INSURANCE	....
HOUSE INSURANCE	....
HP AGREEMENTS	....
OTHER (e.g. medical insurance)	....
TRAVEL	
BUS/RAIL/TUBE FARE	....
CAR COSTS (fuel plus proportion of tax)	....
CAR REPAIR/SERVICING (average)	....
CAR/BIKE INSURANCE	....
CAR BREAKDOWN	....
GOING OUT/PERSONAL SPENDING	
FOOD SHOPPING	....
DRINKS AND/OR CIGARETTES	....
HOBBIES/GYM MEMBERSHIP	....
HAIRCARE/TOILETRIES	....
RESTAURANT MEALS/TAKEAWAYS	....
CLOTHES	....
HOLIDAY	....
OTHER	....

Source: www.moneymadeclear.fsa.gov.uk

good debt advice service that's free of charge (www.cccs.co.uk
or telephone 0800 138 1111). Alternatively, try National Debtline
(www.nationaldebtline.co.uk). Its web site has a useful range of
leaflets that you can download, as well as sample letters to send to
companies to which you owe money. If you prefer, you can contact
it by phoning free on 0808 808 4000.

> Be aware that (at the time of writing) if you type cccs
> into Google, you may get a sponsored link that takes
> you to a company called 'credit card consolidation
> company'. It is *not* CCCS. You get a similar result if you
> type in 'National Debtline'.

One important service these debt advice agencies provide is to help
you work out which debts you should pay off first and how much of
your money creditors may expect to receive. It's absolutely not the
case that you should pay off the company that shouts the loudest.
Often creditors with the fewest rights issue the most threatening
letters.

The debts you should try to prioritize are:

- rent/mortgage (or other loan secured on your home)
- council tax
- gas and electricity
- maintenance or child support
- hire purchase payments
- magistrates' court fines
- TV licence.

I know I've mentioned that you shouldn't pay for someone to sort out your money problems, but I think it deserves repeating. There are dozens of companies that will happily sort out your debt problems if you pay them and others that earn lucrative fees, in some cases for setting up repayment plans that may not be suitable.

Drawing up a repayment budget

This is different from a personal budget, but is designed to help you repay your debts in the right order and in a sustainable way. It's the kind of document you might have to show creditors if you're trying to get them to freeze the interest on your loans. You list money you have to spend (such as on your rent or mortgage) and work out what you have left over for debts.

High interest rates

If you're not at the stage where you're seriously worried about your debts, but recognize that you have some credit card bills or a loan that you want to pay off, you can probably tackle the situation yourself.

Switch your credit cards or loans to a cheaper rate (see page 58) if you're able to and pay off the debt charging the highest rate of interest first. If necessary, pay the minimum on the rest and work your way down.

There are two ways to boost the amount you can pay your creditors or to ensure you have more money left over at the end of the month. The first is to create more money and the second is to spend less. I'll look at creating more money first, as you'll probably find the exercise quite empowering.

Where you can make savings

There are many areas of your everyday spending where you can reduce how much you pay and it doesn't have to take a lot of effort.

Rent

If you live in a rented flat, your scope for cutting down what you pay may be a bit limited. But tenants have become much cannier at working out what the going rate is for their particular kind of property in their area and there's been a definite increase in negotiation.

Mortgage

Competitive mortgage deals will be covered in detail in the next chapter, but if you're paying the standard variable rate on your mortgage, you should definitely consider switching to something cheaper. You may be able to save thousands of pounds a year in payments.

If you're already on a special deal (such as a fixed rate or tracker mortgage) your room for manoeuvre may be limited as you might have to pay expensive redemption penalties to get out of the deal early. Try mortgage brokers' web sites like www.charcol.co.uk or www.lcplc.co.uk to see if you can save money.

Gas and electricity

Whether you're living in a rented property or you own your home, you may be able to save some money by switching to a cheaper energy supplier.

There are so many web sites around that tell you how to save money on your gas and electricity that you might feel you need to shop around for a shopping around web site!

Most make money by taking a commission from the supplier you switch to, and there have been some grumblings about the fact that they don't always compare like with like and calls for a code of practice. All I'd say is that if you have the time, try to get comparison details from two or three sites. I've just done it myself and it took less than five minutes to go through the process on each site.

Energywatch (www.energywatch.org.uk), the web site of the consumer body that deals with complaints about gas and electricity, is a good starting point. It won't recommend a particular supplier, but it will give you an idea of what you could save by switching.

Another useful site is run by the consumer organization Which? (www.switchwithwhich.co.uk). It searches by price and lets you select extra criteria that may be important to you (such as good service, air miles, green energy, etc.).

Others include Moneysupermarket (www.moneysupermarket.com), uSwitch (www.uswitch.com) and Simply Switch (www.simplyswitch.com). All of these (and some others) have signed up to the Energywatch code of conduct, which means they must be impartial and must not favour energy suppliers that pay the most commission.

Landline/mobile/internet

More and more of us are signing up to package deals for landline, broadband and/or mobile phone (sometimes with satellite TV added in as well). The sheer number of bundled deals means it's virtually impossible to compare them accurately and it can mean you're less likely to swap. The best advice is to compare one or two deals and go back to your provider asking it to improve its offer. Providers will often cut the price to keep you as a customer.

Water

You can't pick your water supplier, but you may be able to have a water meter installed, which could save you money. However, not everyone's property is suitable; if you live in a flat or have a shared supply, you may not be able to. If you can, the bigger your property and the fewer people living there, the more you'll save. There's more information on the web sites of the water regulator OFWAT (www.ofwat.gov.uk) or your own water company.

Financial products

The main ones are considered here.

Credit cards

If you owe money on your credit cards, the first thing you should do is to make sure you're paying 0 per cent interest, or the lowest level of interest possible. There are dozens of '0 per cent balance transfer' deals on offer at any one time.

> *In their own words:*
>
> *'We realized that a lot of our money was going on credit card payments. We spent some time finding a 0 per cent deal and set up a standing order to pay off the lot by the time the 0 per cent offer runs out. We'll save so much money.'*

However, many low or 0 per cent deals now come with fees of up to 3 per cent, so if you're thinking of transferring £1812 (the average credit card balance), you may have to pay £54. And just because you're transferring your balance to a 0 per cent deal, it doesn't necessarily mean you pay no interest as you'll normally be charged the standard interest rate on your transfer fee. Happily for credit card companies, they don't miss a trick when it comes to making money!

Store cards

If you've got any store cards in your purse or wallet, cut them up now and tell the card company you're closing your account. It's such an expensive way to go shopping that it's really not worth it.

Bank loan

Switching your bank loan can mean savings, but you may have to pay a redemption penalty. Most banks charge one or two months' interest for paying off a loan early, so, to work out whether it's worth your while, get in touch with the bank and ask how much it would charge or dig out the loan agreement and study the small print.

When you're looking for your new loan, bear in mind that many lenders work out how much interest they'll charge on the basis of your credit report and factors like employment status. Web sites will quote 'typical APRs' which, by law, should mean the interest rate is available to two thirds of the successful applicants. However, you may not know the actual rate you'll be charged until you receive the loan offer.

Payment protection insurance (PPI)

If you want to save money, an easy way to do it is to cancel your payment protection insurance. You should get a percentage of your premiums back and you may be reimbursed everything you paid if you were mis-sold. There are no accurate figures, but experts believe many thousands of consumers were sold policies they didn't want or couldn't claim on.

So, if, for example, you were unemployed or self-employed when you were sold the policy or were told you had to buy it as a condition of the loan and weren't informed you could shop around, you may have a claim.

How do I claim?

Your first step is to complain to the bank or credit card company that sold you the policy. Mark your letter 'formal complaint' to make sure it gets to the right desk. A couple of web sites, including www.thisismoney.co.uk, have templates to help you draft your letter.

If you don't get anywhere with the PPI provider, you can take your complaint to the Financial Ombudsman Service (see details at www.financial-ombudsman.org.uk). It's free for consumers to make a complaint.

Shopping around for PPI

You may have been able to work out that I'm not a fan of PPI, but some people do like to take out loan protection cover. So, if you really think it's something that will be worthwhile, shop around.

The Financial Services Authority plans to introduce (in March 2008) a comparison table for PPI, which is good news if you're trying to find a competitive policy. In the meantime, try these companies for low-cost PPI: British Insurance (www.britishinsurance.com), Paymentcare (www.paymentcare.co.uk) and the Post Office (www.postoffice.co.uk).

Bank account

If you end up overdrawn and pay interest every month, you should definitely make sure you're with a bank that has low interest rates on overdrafts. Obviously, the ideal thing is to be in credit at all times but, depending on how much you owe, that could be a long-term goal.

In the short term, you should give yourself all the help you can. So, look at overdraft arrangement fees and interest charges. Have a search on the internet and see if you can come up with a better deal.

I'll be looking at all the issues involved in buying a house together in Chapter 5, but it's worth bearing in mind that if you and your partner are thinking of taking out a mortgage and buying a home, it's not the best time to change to a new bank. Switching to a different bank can damage your credit rating, so hold off if you're planning to move soon.

If you're in credit more than you're overdrawn, you should focus on the interest rate on balances. It may seem like a hassle to switch to a better rate, especially as banks are notorious for coming up with headline-grabbing deals that don't last as long as a teenager's attention span, but if you keep money in your current account with a low interest rate on balances, move it elsewhere.

If you've paid money in fees for going overdrawn without permission, you may be able to get some of it back. Banks have been under the spotlight for the fees they charge and the Office of Fair Trading is looking at whether these fees are unlawful. In the meantime, thousands of customers have been challenging the banks and getting the fees repaid. If you think you've been unlawfully charged there's a step-by-step guide to reclaiming charges on BBC online (www.bbc.co.uk), which includes letters you can download. Alternatively the Which? web site has its own guide (www.which. co.uk and search on 'bank charges').

Savings account

We all know that we should have our money in a savings account paying a good rate of interest. But sometimes we don't bother to switch. If that rings bells with you, here's some maths to give you a bit of a push:

You have £1000 in an account paying 0.1 per cent. At the end of the year the bank pays you £1 in interest. But worse than that, you then have to pay tax on that interest. So you don't even get a pound for giving the bank the use of your £1000 for 365 days.

Now, suppose you move your £1000 to an account paying 6.25 per cent (at the time of writing there were nine savings accounts paying 6.25 per cent or more). A year later you'll have at least £62.50 in interest. OK, so the taxman will want his slice, but it's still a lot better than a pound.

House insurance

If you rent your property, you can still shop around for contents insurance, but you may not have as much choice as someone who owns their home. You can search online, but if you try you'll probably come up with a load of irrelevant web sites. You might be better off talking to a specialist broker, so to find one who deals with insurance for tenants, you should contact the British Insurance Brokers' Association (BIBA). Log onto its web site (www.biba.org.uk) and click on 'find a broker' or ring its consumer line on 0901 814 0015.

> If you live in a leasehold flat (in England and Wales), you normally have to use the insurance chosen by the landlord or the management company. In Scotland it will state in the title deeds whether you arrange insurance individually or with the other flat owners.

If you own your house it's down to you who insures it. Your mortgage lender can't insist that you take out its own buildings insurance policy but it may charge you an 'admin fee' if you switch your insurance to another provider. Don't worry, because by switching you'll generally save far more than the fee itself.

> If you don't want the hassle of moving to a different company, find out what the competition is charging and contact your insurer threatening to take your business elsewhere. There's no *guarantee* it will work, but insurance is often priced 'elastically' (that's a posh word for saying it's not set in stone) and there's normally room for haggling.

Car insurance

Shopping around for car insurance is worth doing, but don't simply look at the price. Policies do vary quite widely between insurers and you may save a few pounds, but end up with a much higher excess or an inferior policy.

Once again, don't just use one price comparison web site because this can give you quite different results. You could try: www.confused.com, www.moneysupermarket.com and www.uswitch.com, and ring or log onto BIBA (www.biba.org.uk) for details of specialist motor insurance brokers.

How much can you save?

If you've taken your budget and religiously worked your way from top to bottom, switching suppliers, credit card providers and insurers and not resting until you've finished, well done! At the very least hopefully you've made a start and been motivated to carry on by some of the savings you've been able to make.

Now it's your turn to cut down …

This section is more important than switching to save money. It's about you making a conscious decision to spend less and to live within your means. But I wanted you to have a head start by realizing that there were ways you could save money without making huge sacrifices or – in fact – any real sacrifice at all.

So, have a look at what else is in your budget and make a decision about how much you can cut down. It's something that you should do with your partner; if you're spending too much, it's going to affect both of you. Not necessarily immediately and not necessarily because you'll find the bailiffs at your front door, but if you are living a lifestyle that you can't afford, it will catch up with you one day. And if you're living that lifestyle, it's probably already causing you stress.

I don't think it's helpful to give you a list of ways you can cut down your spending (taking sandwiches to work instead of buying them, walking to work rather than catching the bus or having instant coffee rather than your daily latte from Costa-bucks). You'll know from your spending diary where the money is going. What's important is to feel you want to live within your budget.

In their own words:

'I didn't realize how much my partner and I were spending on treats. I thought it was just a few pounds a week, but sometimes it was £20 or £30. It was something we could easily cut down.'

One last money-raising tip: sell things you don't need on eBay or through ads in your local paper. Depending on what it is, you could really be quids in.

Women: money managers or the Cinderella complex?

Historically, it's often been women who've made the decisions about money. That's not true across all cultures and in all situations, but many women have made sure the bills were paid and dealt with day-to-day money.

Today, some women still have control of the finances, but there are others who are happy to leave all the financial decisions to their husband or partner, and a small number who expect their partner to 'rescue' them.

The woman with the 'Cinderella complex' may overspend without any thought of how she'll pay off the debt, because she thinks her man will save the day. This fondness for overspending has been fuelled by the celebrity culture. Magazines tell us how to look like a celebrity and – sometimes – how to spend like one as well.

In February 2007, one debt company found that women in the 20–35 age group who asked it for advice owed more than £23,000 on average. A staggering 93 per cent of this was credit or store card debt and 80 per cent of the women said they felt under pressure to shop when they didn't have the money, to keep up with either friends and colleagues or celebrities.

I'm not trying to trivialize why women get into debt. Some genuinely can't make ends meet and others make decisions which may have been understandable at the time, but which later come back to haunt them. However, some women are happy to indulge in retail therapy and even happier to let their man pay the bill if and when they can't.

How does it damage your relationship?

Relate counsellors deal with a lot of relationship problems that either have their roots in money issues, or manifest themselves in the way the couple deal with money. So what starts as a money problem can become a relationship problem. Someone who expects their partner to pick up the tab every time their credit card bill gets too high could, at first sight, appear to be relinquishing control of part of their life. It may seem like they want someone to look after them. But you could see it another way.

The person who expects their partner to bail them out isn't taking ownership of their own decisions. Relate goes so far as to describe this behaviour as 'abusive' in some situations, particularly if there's been secrecy around money and debts.

Men aren't angels either!

Increasingly, financial advisers and debt counsellors say they see young men who have their own well-developed financial weakness. It's more likely to be going out, gadgets or even a new car, rather than clothes or shoes.

Debt counsellors I spoke to said that when young men come to see them for advice, they may be behind on all their credit agreements, but their car loan is often up to date. And sometimes men can be less concerned with the details and can be bigger risk-takers, which means that they can owe more than women when they get into debt.

It's absolutely not the case that men are better than women at managing money or vice versa. But it is true to say that men and women have different ways of dealing with money; each has their own strengths and weaknesses. Again, not all women and men conform to type (by a long way), but if you're aware of these money management patterns, it can help make sense of your partner's behaviour or your own.

> If you're with someone who wants to be rescued from their debts, be wary about agreeing to bail them out without giving them some financial 'lesson' or a plan of action, otherwise you're setting up a pattern of behaviour, where you are always on hand to sort out their financial mess.

Mine or ours?

You and your partner may have different ideas about where the cuts should come, but another factor that will determine how much you decide on your budget jointly is the extent to which you combine your money. That will depend on your personal attitudes and possibly on whether or not you are married. Research by Alliance & Leicester bank found that one in three single people say they'll keep their finances separate and have no plans to open a joint account.

The research also found that:

- 8 per cent of those in a relationship didn't trust their partner enough to share their finances

- 28 per cent didn't want to have a joint account, but to keep all their money separate

- 41 per cent had never brought up the subject; they just kept their money separate and kept quiet about it

- 17 per cent thought sharing their money would lead to arguments.

How much to share

There's no prescriptive way to do this, but you might want to start with a joint account to cover your bills. Work out how much each of you is going to contribute. If one of you is earning £800 a month and the other is earning £3000, it's not fair to split the contribution 50:50.

> *In their own words:*
>
> *'We both have a separate account and one joint one. As I'm currently on maternity leave, I'm not paying anything into it, but I have got a little bit put by so I can still spend "my" money.'*

You may begin to feel comfortable pooling more of your money the longer you're together. As long as you're both happy with what you're doing and why you're doing it, that's fine. But keep a check on your motivation for making changes. For example, you shouldn't pool your money if you're really using it as a control mechanism – it won't work and your partner will resent it.

Here are your choices:

- separate accounts
- joint account for bills and separate accounts for your own spending
- joint accounts.

Separate accounts

Many couples, particularly those who cohabit rather than marry, start out their life together with separate accounts. And for some it stays that way. There's even a name for it: SALTies or people with Separate Accounts Living Together. The problem with keeping your money separate is that it can make it easier to keep secrets.

What you avoid by keeping your money separate is any liability for your partner's debts. And because you each have control over 'your money' you may keep on top of it more than if you each thought it was the other's responsibility to sort out a joint account. Just make sure you each contribute to the bills in a fair way.

> *In their own words:*
>
> *'We've been married for two years and have a baby, but we keep our money completely separate. If you'd told me a few years ago I'd be doing that when I was married I'd have thought it really strange, but it works well for us and we still think of the money as "ours".'*

Joint and separate accounts

Opening a joint account for bills and having separate accounts for spending money is definitely becoming more popular both among those who live together and married couples. Many couples feel that it gives them the best of both worlds: the means of sharing the cost of the bills and the chance to have some financial independence.

It's important that both of you see the bills so you both know how much it costs to run your home. It can be hard to know why you're being asked for £400 a month if you don't realize how it all adds up. As before, splitting the cost equitably should be a priority.

In their own words:

'I think with hindsight it would have been better if we'd contributed to shared bills on the basis of our earnings, rather than 50:50. I had to work much harder than Malcolm to pay 50 per cent of everything and he couldn't acknowledge this, which was a cause of tension.'

Joint accounts

The advantage of sharing everything in a joint account is that you both know exactly what's going on. It keeps your finances simple as you don't have to juggle your accounts and it automatically makes it easier to think of whatever you have as 'our money' not 'yours and mine'. But the openness can be a disadvantage as well in that it makes it harder to buy surprise presents or treats for your partner (or for you!) if your partner expects you to justify every penny spent. It can cause tension if you both live by different rules.

However, the real disadvantage is that if one of you runs up debts, you're each liable for the whole lot (not just half). So if the relationship goes wrong, you could have a large debt to pay or the prospect of major damage to your credit rating.

In their own words:

'We share all our money in a joint account. Originally we had separate accounts as well, but it all seemed too complicated. I think marriage is about sharing anyway, so it's not an issue.'

Strategies for dealing with money differences

Whatever your differences, you must each be prepared to compromise, which can be easy to say, but harder to do. But if you don't, you'll only resent your partner's habits and your frustrations are likely to affect other areas of your relationship.

Talk about money

The idea is that you talk – and listen. If you have different ideas about money, try to work towards a situation where the saver can do the saving and the spender can spend (within limits) without worrying about being criticized.

Don't make assumptions

Don't jump to conclusions about your partner's spending patterns. Be prepared to find out what's really going on. Some people – and this can be a particular problem for women who've given up work to look after their children – complain that they have to account for every penny. They're sometimes made to feel that they've got a bad shopping habit, when really they're spending very little.

Take responsibility

Don't get into the habit of pointing the finger of blame: 'If you hadn't spent so much on the plasma TV, we'd be fine,' or 'You don't let us take a holiday'. You should each be prepared to take responsibility for your share of the financial decisions. If one partner controls the relationship through money it could become emotionally abusive, but that could also apply if one partner refuses to take any responsibility for the financial decisions they make.

Accept each other's financial limits

If one of you earns a lot more than the other, it could be a source of conflict. If you earn less you may feel angry if your partner splashes out on treats in a way you can't, or you may worry if they want to pay for holidays or expensive meals out. But don't feel you have to try to match them pound for pound.

Be honest

Most of us tell 'little white lies' from time to time, but you should be honest about what's coming in and what's going out. Tell your partner how your own financial decisions make you feel, what you'd like to change about yourself, and what you find difficult about what they do and don't do.

Spend less, save more

Living within your budget doesn't just mean spending every penny. Once you've paid off your debts, you should start a savings account. If you've already got one, could you increase the amount you pay into it? If you don't think you need to save, ask yourself what you would do if you (or your partner) couldn't work for a month.

Most people who get into debt do so because there's an unexpected 'life event' such as redundancy, illness, divorce or a bereavement. Few of us would be able to save enough to cushion ourselves from the financial effects of long-term illness or redundancy (there are ways you can insure against that, which I'll talk about in Chapter 8), but in the meantime, knowing you have some money to fall back on will make you feel more confident about the future. And when you feel confident, you make better decisions.

CHAPTER 5

A roof over your head

For many couples buying a home together is seen as a big emotional as well as a financial commitment. It shows your relationship is solid. But if house prices are rising faster than wages, you may find you are bounced into buying a home with your partner before you feel ready.

Research by the Halifax bank in 2007 showed that in over 90 per cent of towns and cities around the UK the price of an average property was too expensive for first-time buyers. So an obvious way to get round this problem is to team up with your partner. Or is it? It's a question that only you and your partner can really know the answer to. But before you take things any further, it's probably a good idea to have a look at the pros and cons.

The pros
Buying a home together now could be a good idea if the following apply.

1. You know that sharing your space can work
It's not just about whether your partner spends hours in the bathroom, leaves their clothes all over the bedroom floor or thinks the washing up should be done only when you're down to the last plate. You may have very different ideas about how you spend time in your home and even what you want it to look like. If you already

know that living together works well, it's one less thing to worry about.

> Try living together. If it means you have a better understanding of what it could be like when you buy a place of your own, it's a useful exercise.

In their own words:

'When I first met Adam, it seemed like a real commitment to take out a joint mortgage and it took a few years of living together in a rented flat to get to the stage where we felt confident about it.'

2. You already have a deposit or you're on the way

If you have a deposit, you have a head start. It shows you're disciplined enough to set aside money from your salary and it means you'll be able to get better mortgage deals than someone with no savings.

> Get a deposit of at least 5 per cent; 10 per cent is better because it gives you access to more of the really competitive mortgage deals. It also means you will be less likely to pay an extra charge for borrowing a high percentage of the property's value (called a higher lending charge). The fee for a higher lending charge is typically around £2000 and it's designed to cover the lender in case you default on your mortgage. However, not all lenders charge it (Nationwide is one of the bigger lenders not to do so).

3. You could afford the mortgage

If you're already renting separately or if you each own a property, you should save money by buying together and if you already rent together you *may* find that a mortgage wouldn't cost much more.

> Make sure you include all the extras: research by Alliance & Leicester found that the total cost of moving for first-time buyers was over £7600 (excluding the deposit). This included £4600 on furniture and white goods such as a fridge and washing machine. Your monthly budget may be a little more stretched than you anticipate.

4. You feel comfortable about taking on a mortgage with your partner

This is a tricky one because there are no guarantees in life and in some ways you won't know what your partner will be like as a co-owner until you take the plunge. But you'll probably have had some clues if they are going to be a complete disaster.

> During your time together you should have been able to build up a fairly good picture of what your partner is like with money and what their attitude to a major financial commitment like a mortgage is going to be. If you've already had a conversation about managing the mortgage, you're doing well.

In their own words:

'I wanted to spend more on a house at the time and my partner wanted to pay less and move again in about ten years' time, but there were no arguments. We sat down and came to a compromise.'

The cons

On the other hand, I wouldn't recommend a trip to the estate agent's office just yet if any of these apply to you.

1. You think owning a home together will improve your relationship

If you think your relationship will be cemented by the financial ties of a joint mortgage, you're sadly mistaken. Unless you resolve the problems around your relationship first, buying a home together would probably only highlight any difficulties that already exist.

> There may never be a 'perfect' time to buy a house together, but don't use it as a solution to a problem in your relationship.

2. You would struggle to afford the mortgage on both your incomes

If you know that buying a home together would put a big strain on your finances, don't do it. Most first-time buyers find the first year or two hard going financially, not least because of all the 'extras' that come with buying property. They could include:

Costs of purchasing a home:

- stamp duty: nothing on a property up to £125,000; 1 per cent of the purchase price on a property between £125,001 and £250,000; 3 per cent on the £250,001 to £500,000 band; and 4 per cent on the £500,001+ band

- legal fees: £1400 on average

- survey fees: a homebuyer's survey is about £400 for a £125,000 property and £545 for a £300,000 property; a building survey is about £550 for a £125,000 property and £750 for a £300,000 property

- removal costs: these can be £500 to £1000+.

Additional monthly costs include:

- council tax: a band A property is about £940 per annum and a band D one about £1410

- household and contents insurance can be £200–£400

- life insurance upwards of £20 a month.

> Stop looking at property web sites and dig out your bank statements for the past few months. Look at how much each of you spends and what you spend your money on. Can you make savings (see Chapter 4) if you need to?
>
> If you don't know how much you'd need to pay each month, look at an affordability calculator on the internet. Many mortgage brokers and lenders have them. Try Charcol (www.charcol.co.uk) or London and Country (www.lcplc.co.uk). If the mortgage is more than you're currently paying in rent, set aside the difference for 3–6 months and see how it feels. Can you really afford it? If not, don't buy.

3. Your job is not very secure

Job security is a complex concept these days as we can earn an income in many different ways. However, there's a difference between realizing you've not got a job for life and having a strong feeling that you may be made redundant or that your contract may not be renewed.

> Wait until your income situation becomes clearer or more secure. If you decide to leave your job and move to a different employer, you may find it harder to get a mortgage if you have to complete a probationary period and/or if you're changing direction.

4. You don't have any savings

Some mortgage lenders – although far fewer since the 2007 'credit crunch' – will let you borrow 100 per cent of the property's value. You'll need to have some cash for all the extras I mentioned above, but you don't actually *need* money in the bank to put down as a deposit.

Having said that, it's not something I'd advise you to do. Why not? First, you won't get the best mortgage deals and second, if house prices fall you could find yourself in negative equity, where you owe more than the value of your property.

> You have two options:
> a)   borrowing or being given the money from someone else (like generous parents) or
> b)   saving the money yourself,
>   but it's always better to have some savings of your own.

In their own words:

'When I bought a flat with Philip, his mum and dad helped with the deposit. But they then felt they had the right to tell us what we should buy and where. That was quite difficult to deal with.'

You've decided to buy – what next?

Whether you're a first- or a second-time buyer, the key to happy home ownership is preparation, preparation, preparation. It's particularly important if there's a queue of buyers for every flat or house, but it's a good idea whatever the housing market is doing.

When I talked to estate agents and solicitors about how first-time buyers can get ahead, they all said the same: sort out your mortgage in advance. If you already own property then try to sell it before you start looking.

Sorting out your finance in advance

This normally means getting a mortgage 'agreement in principle', where the mortgage lender tells you how much it is prepared to lend you both, based on information you've provided and credit checks it has carried out. It doesn't guarantee you'll be able to borrow that amount as it will depend on the valuation of the property you want to buy and further credit checks when you actually sign up to the loan.

An agreement in principle will:

- tell you how much you can borrow

- let sellers know that you have the ability to borrow the mortgage you need

- let you find out whether you have any credit issues that could cause a problem with a mortgage application.

Before you start thinking about applying for an agreement in principle, I would advise you to get hold of a copy of your credit file from each of the three credit reference agencies – Equifax, Experian and Call Credit – as I outlined in Chapter 2.

Getting an agreement in principle

You will have to give information such as how much you will be able to put down as a deposit, what your gross monthly income is and what your debts are (including credit card debts and personal loans).

You can do this over the internet, by phone or by visiting your local mortgage broker or lender. It's much easier and cheaper to do it over the internet, but you may be missing out on some useful advice. Many mortgage brokers offer different levels of service. I'll explain what to look for in a broker, and what they cost, a little later on.

One word of warning

If you are planning on shopping around for the best mortgage online, make sure you don't damage your credit record. If you apply for an agreement in principle, the mortgage lender will carry out a credit check and when that happens, it is logged on your credit file (called a 'footprint' in the jargon). Some lenders leave a 'hard' footprint, which can be seen by other lenders, others a 'soft' footprint, which cannot. A mortgage broker should be able to guide you through the footprint maze.

If you have half a dozen checks, because you've been shopping around for the best deal, the footprint could cause a problem. Lenders see multiple credit checks as either a sign that someone is taking on a lot of debt or that they are applying for loans fraudulently. You need only one agreement in principle so don't apply for several by mistake. The mortgage lender or broker's site should warn you at the point at which your credit record will be checked.

> You don't have to apply for an agreement in principle with the mortgage lender you finally go with. Some mortgage brokers advise borrowers to apply for an agreement in principle with a lender that leaves a soft footprint. Once you have found the property you want, you can always apply for a mortgage with another lender and your credit file will not be any the worse for it.

How will you pay for your home?

The two big decisions you will have to make are how you are going to pay for your home (i.e. what kind of mortgage you will have) and how you are going to own it. Let's look at how you are going to pay for it first, as that's the decision you will need to invest more time and effort in.

In most cases, buying a home means taking out a mortgage. The word 'mortgage' has its origins in ancient French and it means 'pledge until death'. Not the kind of thought you want rattling around your brain while you're looking for your dream home.

The point is that a mortgage is a pretty grown-up financial contract. Thinking about how you're going to pay back the money you borrow isn't going to set your heart racing. But signing up for a duff deal will mean you have less money to spend on what you want, or even on day-to-day basics.

You'll probably have noticed that there's plenty of information available about mortgages, especially on the internet, but not all these sources are impartial. A lot of information is produced by companies hoping to sell you something, whereas if you're reading this book, you'll already have bought it (or someone else has) so there's no commercial agenda here.

Assessing the mortgage options

Joint mortgage

Assuming that both of you are earning, you'll probably want to take out a joint mortgage, because you can borrow more than a solo buyer. The amount that banks and building societies are prepared to lend buyers has been creeping up over the years because many believe that, despite some rises, interest rates are likely to remain at *relatively* low levels for the foreseeable future.

How much can you borrow?

As a rough guide, you should be able to borrow a minimum of four times your joint incomes (although you may be able to borrow more) depending on your credit rating and any other debts you have. Be aware that the 'credit crunch' of 2007 has made some lenders more cautious.

However, some lenders are changing the way they calculate how much they lend. It's goodbye 'income multiples' and hello 'affordability'. Affordability means the lender will take into account how much you pay each month in loans, council tax, etc., as well as your income. They'll also have a close look at your credit score, which is different to your credit record. The credit record simply shows how you have managed any money you've borrowed.

The credit score is a system that lenders have devised to show how good or bad a risk you might be. The problem is that it's pretty difficult to predict exactly what will give you a better credit score as each company takes different factors into account. But there are some things that will definitely count against you:

- 🐷 **If you are not on the electoral roll.**
- 🐷 **If you have recently changed job.**
- 🐷 **If you have recently moved house.**
- 🐷 **If you have recently changed your bank account.**

By now you'll have worked out that mortgage lenders don't really like change. They prefer you to have stuck with your bank account for a few years (although anything over ten years doesn't affect your score) when you apply for your mortgage. If you need to bump up your credit score, you could consider taking out a credit card (especially if you don't have one), but *only* if you will pay it off in full each month. Don't take on more debt.

> If you want to switch banks, you can still do so and keep your credit score intact if you don't close down the original account. You have to be honest in your mortgage application, but it would be quite acceptable to apply for an account with your new bank and run it in tandem with your old one until your mortgage has been arranged.

If you've got a blemish on your financial record that you've been trying to ignore or cover up, now's the time to confront it. Don't bury your head in the sand because the lender will find out anyway. One mortgage broker told me if there's something in your financial history that you think may be a problem, it is far less likely to cause difficulties with your mortgage application if you tell the prospective lender first.

In their own words:

'When we applied for our mortgage, Susan had some credit cards that she'd got behind on years ago. We were really worried that it would cause problems, but luckily it didn't. It was a pretty stressful time though.'

The mortgage application process

An increasing number of mortgage lenders do most of their applications online, which means the process will be faster and you can monitor its progress. To speed everything up, get hold of your last three months' payslips and your last three months' bank statements. Lenders do scrutinize these carefully and if the evidence from your bank statements doesn't match what you've said on your application form, you may have some explaining to do.

If you're self-employed

If one or both of you is self-employed, your application should be straightforward as long as you can prove your income. Lenders normally insist on two years' worth of accounts (or one year's accounts and a forecast), which may be a problem if you have set up your business relatively recently. If your accountant has managed to reduce your income for tax purposes then that may be a problem if you want a large loan.

This is where a broker can be invaluable, but – as with most things in life – there are good and bad ones out there. A good one won't just find the best mortgage deal for you but will also take into account factors like whether the mortgage lender takes a sympathetic approach if you are self-employed, or whether it is less flexible.

Because the mortgage broker will have built up its own track record with the lender, it can sometimes get you a mortgage more easily if you are self-employed or have a portfolio of contract jobs than you could if you approached the lender directly.

Paying back the loan

These days most borrowers take out a repayment mortgage, but not so long ago (before the endowment mis-selling scandal surfaced), interest-only loans were far more popular.

Repayment mortgage

A repayment mortgage lets you pay back a bit of the original capital you borrowed, plus the interest you owe, every month, so it's the safest way of repaying your mortgage because it's guaranteed. As long as you make every payment you are supposed to, the money you borrowed will be paid back at the end of the term. But not all repayment loans are the same.

Some lenders adjust the amount you owe only once a year (it's called calculating annual interest) so even though you pay your mortgage every month, your balance only reduces annually. It effectively makes these lenders' loans more expensive. Happily, most do reduce the balance every day.

Interest-only mortgages

With an interest-only mortgage you don't pay the original amount you borrowed, just the interest, so you need a separate policy or plan to generate enough to clear the debt. Many people don't like the idea that the amount they owe the bank never goes down and there's invariably some risk that you may not be able to pay it all off.

Payment options

The main ones are:

1. *Regular payments:* It's not a structured way of paying your loan, but it's quite popular with high earners in the city. They simply use some or all of their annual bonus to reduce the outstanding balance every year. But it's a high-risk move if your bonus isn't consistent or you aren't disciplined. Be careful.

2. *Individual Savings Account (ISA):* ISAs are a way of investing your money without paying tax on the proceeds. You can pay £7000 a year into an ISA that invests in share-based funds each year, so if you have a joint mortgage, that means £14,000. However, because the ISA invests in shares, which as we all know can go down as well as up, there's no guarantee your ISA will perform well enough to pay off the loan in full.

3. *Endowments:* Because of the fallout from the endowment mis-selling scandal you're unlikely to be recommended an endowment as a way of repaying your loan. They're expensive because you pay all the commission and charges upfront; they're not very flexible, because they run for a fixed period (normally 10, 15 or 25 years);

and, most importantly, there's no guarantee that your mortgage will be paid off. Now you see why endowment mortgages are not a good idea.

4. *Pension:* Pension mortgages have fallen out of favour for similar reasons. The idea is that if you have a private pension (as opposed to an occupational scheme), you can use some of the money you've saved into your pension fund to pay off your home loan when you retire. But bearing in mind that most people don't save enough for their retirement in the first place, it's not really practical and I'd be pretty wary of an adviser who recommended such a scheme.

Which mortgage rate?

Once you've decided how you are going to pay back the money you want to borrow, you need to think about the interest rate. The UK has one of the most competitive mortgage markets in the world, which means you should be able to get a good deal.

Here are your options:

- standard variable rate
- fixed rate
- tracker rate
- discount rate
- capped rate
- cashback mortgage.

Standard variable rate (SVR)

Avoid this option at all costs. It's never used by banks or building societies to tempt buyers with and is normally 1.5–2 per cent higher than the Bank of England base rate. It doesn't always fall by as much as the base rate does when it falls and can rise by more when it increases.

Fixed rate

This will give you the most security about how much you pay as the rate is fixed for the duration of the mortgage deal. You often have to pay an early redemption penalty or charge, but if a rise in interest rates would cause a problem to your monthly budget, it's a good option.

Many lenders offer two- and five-year fixed rate deals, but you can get longer-term fixes. Sometimes fixed rates seem expensive compared with other mortgage deals, normally when further interest rate rises are expected.

If you go to a mortgage or price comparison web site and look at the top five tracker and top five fixed rate deals, you'll be able to work out how much more you would pay and whether it's worth it.

Tracker rate

The concept of a tracker rate is simple: it tracks the Bank of England base rate. So, if the base rate rises by 0.25 per cent, so does the tracker, but that doesn't mean that all tracker deals are the same as the bank or building society makes its profit through a mark-up.

Looking at a handful of mortgages on offer in 2007, two-year deals ranged from 0.8 per cent below base rate to just 0.1 per cent below base rate, which on a £200,000 mortgage works out at a difference of £115 a month.

In their own words:

'We've got slightly different ideas about the mortgage. I'm more cautious than Andy and would normally go for a fixed rate, so one time we split the mortgage, 50 per cent tracker and 50 per cent fixed.'

Discount rate

At first sight a discount rate looks pretty similar to a tracker. It's lower than the lender's ordinary variable rate and it goes up and down when interest rates rise and fall. But there is a difference: a discount rate is directly linked to a lender's standard variable rate, not the Bank of England base rate.

So if your lender is excruciatingly slow to lower its standard variable rate and quick to raise it, your discount rate will do the same. And there's another complication: the level of SVRs can vary quite widely between lenders. So, a discount mortgage set at 1.65 per cent below one lender's SVR, where the SVR is 7.65 per cent, will be cheaper than one at 1.75 per cent below the SVR if that rate is 7.9 per cent.

Capped rate

The capped rate seems to deliver the best of both worlds. Your mortgage is capped at a certain level, so you know the maximum you'll ever have to pay, but if interest rates fall, then your mortgage could reduce as well. The problem is that not many lenders offer them, so your choice could be pretty limited.

Some lenders link their capped rates to the SVR, others base theirs on a tracker rate. It's an important difference and normally a mortgage that's based on a tracker rate will be cheaper.

Cashback mortgage

This may look tempting if you are strapped for cash when you are buying your home – and let's face it, who isn't? When you complete the mortgage deal, you receive a cash sum that you can spend on exactly what you like. However, you normally pay for the upfront cash several times over during the lifetime of the deal through higher interest rates.

What other factors should you consider?

Don't just think about the interest rate – you may want your mortgage to have extra flexibility as well to cope with unexpected or anticipated future events.

Flexible mortgage

Most mortgages have some flexibility built in, but a truly flexible mortgage will let you make overpayments, reduce payments and even stop paying your mortgage altogether for a few months. It will also calculate interest on a daily basis and let you borrow back money you've overpaid. You can get flexible fixed rate deals, trackers and capped rates, etc.

Offset mortgage

The idea of an offset mortgage is that instead of having a mortgage, where you're charged interest on the whole debt and money in a savings account (where you pay tax on the interest you earn), you have both with the same mortgage lender and your savings are used to offset what you owe on your mortgage. The result? You effectively owe less money, pay less tax and your mortgage term is shortened.

Because offset mortgages don't normally have the very best

rates you need at least 8 per cent of the outstanding mortgage balance in savings for the maths to add up.

Self-certification mortgage

These mortgages sound a bit too good to be true: you tell the lender how much you earn, but you don't have to prove it. However, for some people they are the only way to get a home loan. If you're self-employed but haven't been trading for long enough to have two years' worth of accounts you may find it hard to get an ordinary mortgage. Likewise if you're employed on a contract basis with less than six months to go but don't have a follow-up contract lined up.

You normally have to put down a larger deposit than with an ordinary residential mortgage: 10 per cent is usually the absolute minimum and 15 per cent is not unusual. You won't get the best deals with a self-certification mortgage either. With a 15 per cent deposit you'd normally expect to pay a premium of 0.5 per cent above the 'normal' interest rate.

Sub-prime or adverse credit mortgage

Another reason why you may not be able to get a mainstream mortgage is if you have unpaid debts or a county court judgment. This is where the sub-prime or adverse credit lenders, which specialize in lending money to people who have a poor credit history, can step in.

But, you pay a higher interest rate and you should be *very* careful, as although there are some recognized names operating in the sub-prime market, there are some unscrupulous companies as well. They are often happy to lend money, knowing that if the borrower can't keep up the payments their home could be repossessed – and some are very quick to take repossession action.

Don't assume that because you've had debt problems you won't be able to borrow from a high street lender. That may not be the case and it's something a good mortgage broker would be able to advise you on.

Using a mortgage broker

There are thousands of mortgage brokers around so finding one isn't difficult. But for them to be able to get the best deal, they must be truly independent and have access to mortgage deals from the whole market. A good mortgage broker should:

- get you a good deal to suit your specific circumstances

- recommend a lender who is good at processing applications and doing the admin, not just one with a competitive rate

- take into account issues like flexibility and upfront charges

- do a lot of the chasing on your behalf

Word of mouth is often a good way of finding one, otherwise I'd suggest looking at the personal finance pages of the papers (either online or offline) to see who's regularly quoted in mortgage-related articles. They're not being endorsed by the publication, but normally journalists will try to quote someone who's respected in their field. Avoid a mortgage broker who's tied to an estate agent if you can because:

- many of them use a 'panel' of mortgage lenders, which means they restrict themselves to (typically) a few dozen different banks and building societies, while some brokers use as few as nine lenders

- the broker could be in a position where they can pass information to the estate agent about how much you can afford. It's illegal for estate agents to imply that you're more likely to get the property you're after if you use their mortgage broker – but that doesn't stop some pushy agents from doing that

- they don't generally rely on repeat business, so there isn't the same incentive for them to go the extra mile.

> When you're choosing a mortgage broker, ask them whether they look at the whole market or operate a panel of lenders. If they adopt the latter option, ask them how many mortgage lenders make up the panel. It's information they're obliged to give you.

Paying for a mortgage broker

Some brokers charge a fee of up to 1 per cent of the loan (although a more typical level is 0.4–0.5 per cent), some charge a standard flat fee (of typically a few hundred pounds) and others take a commission directly from the lender.

An independent mortgage broker will give you the option of paying a fee if you prefer and they must tell you how much they will charge for their advice.

Mortgage fees

These are different to mortgage broker fees, but are linked to the mortgage deal itself. Not so long ago you would expect to pay a couple of hundred pounds as an arrangement fee and possibly another £400–£500 if you were taking out a fixed rate mortgage. These days you can easily spend more than £1000 and sometimes over £2000 on arrangement fees.

Generally, the shorter the term of the mortgage deal, the more important the level of the fees is. If you've signed up to a two-year mortgage deal with fees of £1000, that's £500 a year. If it's a five-year deal, it's only £200 a year. Also, the smaller your mortgage, the better it is to opt for a low or no-fee deal.

Buying your home

OK, so you've thought about how you're going to pay for your home and you may even have started looking. There's a long way to go before you're homeowners, but you're definitely on the path. The vast majority of couples who buy a property together do so jointly so both their names appear on the deeds, but there are different ways of owning your home together.

When you go and see your conveyancing solicitor, who will help you with the house-buying process, they will run through the options for you. Once you have decided how you both want to own your home, you will normally be asked to confirm this in writing so there is a record of your decision. There are three options – joint tenants, tenants in common or sole ownership.

Joint tenants

If you own your property as joint tenants, you split it equally between you. It's important to be clear about this, because the 50:50 split is not affected by how much each of you pays towards the mortgage. It also means that when one of you dies, your share of the property automatically passes to the other partner (even if this is not written in your will or you haven't made one).

Tenants in common

If you own as tenants in common you can decide between you how you want ownership of your home to be split. So, if you contribute different amounts to the deposit and mortgage, you could decide that one of you will own 60 per cent of the property and the other will own the remaining 40 per cent. You must draw up a declaration of trust to spell it out. It's something your solicitor should raise with you and it should cost between £100 and £200.

The other major difference between tenancy in common and joint tenancy is that when you die, the part of the property that you own as a tenant in common becomes part of your estate. There are two ways of looking at this. One is that you have more control over where your share of the property goes when you die: it does not automatically pass to your partner. The other side of the same coin is that it could end up being passed to your family and not to your partner unless you draw up a will.

Most couples, whether married or not, end up buying their home as joint tenants. However, there are specific situations where it will make sense to own a home as tenants in common; the main one is where the partners earn very different salaries and want ownership of the property to reflect that.

Another example is where one partner (or their parents) has provided the deposit, which they want to safeguard. Couples who are on their second marriage and who have children from a previous marriage would also be advised to buy a property as tenants in common.

If you have a *declaration of trust*, you can always alter the percentages of the property you own, should your circumstances change. You can either draw up a new declaration or have an alteration ('addendum' in legal-speak) added to the original one. As well as setting out who owns what, the declaration of trust should state what will happen to the property should the relationship break down. It normally means that one partner should have the opportunity to buy the other one out.

Sole ownership

You may be moving in together without buying a property together. You might be moving into your partner's home, or one of you may be buying the property in their sole name. Perhaps one of you already owns a flat or house which you would rather hang onto than sell. There are some quite straightforward reasons why it may seem like a logical move to buy the property in one person's name.

The buying process

England, Wales and Northern Ireland

Buying a property is rarely straightforward. Although buyers now have more upfront information where Home Information Packs (HIPs) are available in England and Wales, there are still plenty of opportunities for things to go wrong.

It is well worth getting a detailed survey and not relying on the mortgage valuation when you buy. At the very least I would recommend you have a 'homebuyer's report and valuation' and, if you are buying an old property, a 'building survey' (which used to be called a structural survey). Nothing's definite until contracts have been exchanged, which, incidentally, is when you take over responsibility for insuring the property.

Scotland

Scotland uses an 'offers over' process, which means you offer a percentage (typically 20 per cent or more) over the asking price. You have a survey before you make an offer, and if there's more than one buyer interested in the property, it can go to sealed bids, which means you have no idea what you're up against. One advantage of the system is that once your offer has been accepted, it's very difficult for the seller to accept a rival offer.

Winning in the house-buying process

The internet is playing an increasingly important role in the house-selling and buying process, but most people still use an estate agent. The agent's loyalties will be with the seller, because they are paying the agent's commission, but you can still get them on your side:

- Get your finance in place – this means an agreement in principle.

- Do your research. The internet makes it all pretty easy, but several estate agents told me that buyers don't do their research with their 'practical' heads on. You should be asking yourself whether the area you're moving to will supply your needs at a price you can afford.

- Save your arguments for home! Don't waste the agent's time arguing about whether you like the property or not. That's something you can do in the comfort of your own space.

CHAPTER 6

Growing what you have

We all have financial dreams and goals, whether it is to be able to give up work at 50, to buy a house in our favourite holiday destination or to add some extra space to our home. If you think about when you have managed to save the most money, it's probably been when you've had something specific to aim for. What this chapter is going to do is help you to get closer to your dream – whatever it is. And the first step on the way is to decide where you want to be.

In terms of how you invest your money to make it grow to reach your financial goal, it doesn't necessarily matter whether you're saving for a second home or to travel for a year. Whilst the financial services industry does sell a baffling array of products, it doesn't have specific 'second home' or 'year off' investment policies (but give it time and I'm sure it will). What you need to sort out between you is what your financial goals are and how you want to prioritize them.

In their own words:

'Rob didn't mind spending loads on luxury holidays and eating out, whereas I would have preferred a new sofa or bookshelves, something to make the home look nice. It caused tension because we weren't aiming for the same thing.'

You want a new car, I want a new house!

If you have very different ideas about what you want from your money in the longer term, you may have to invest a bit of time in the art of compromise. You've probably had to compromise on all kinds of things throughout your relationship and you'll know it isn't always easy. But for you to build on your wealth as a couple, it's worth doing.

So, ask yourselves:

- What do we want to achieve? How do we see ourselves in a few years' time, in ten years' time and when we've retired?

- Is there anything we particularly want to do which would mean we'd have to put financial plans in place – such as paying off the mortgage at 50 or sending our children to private schools?

- What would we need to do in financial terms to achieve this? You may not be able to work out exact figures, but you'd know whether you needed to save a bit more or come up with a lot of money.

- What have we managed to put in place so far?

- Are we happy with what we've done or do we want to make changes?

- Do we know whether money we've already saved or invested is working hard?

- Have we established how much risk we're prepared to take as a couple, as opposed to our individual attitudes to risk?

> One of you will probably naturally take the lead in your finances. That's understandable, but it shouldn't be used as a way of taking over. When it comes to long-term goals, meeting each other halfway is the key.

Saving v investing

You can't work out how you feel about investing your money until you understand what it involves. Investing isn't the same as saving, but that's not always made clear by financial companies. Confusingly they often call investment plans 'savings plans' when they're not.

If you save money, you earn interest on the original amount you paid in and as time goes on, you earn interest on that interest as well (through 'compounding'). But the value of the original amount you paid in doesn't change and you can always get it back if you need to.

If you invest money, its value can fall or rise. So, if you put £3000 into a share-based fund and the stock market fell, it might only be worth £2500 or even £2000. On the other hand, if share prices rocketed away, it could have grown to £3500 or even £4000. What matters is that the money you've invested isn't guaranteed to keep its initial value.

Investing – a battle of the sexes?

Financial advisers tell me that when they see a couple together, there is often a big difference in the way that men and women save and invest. So, if you understand each other's approach, you'll have a better chance of being able to reach an agreement on a way forward that works for you both.

Research published in the *International Journal of Bank Marketing* (in 2002) revealed two major differences between men and women when it comes to the way they invest.

1.   **Women are less likely than men to take a risk.**

2.   **Women are less confident about the investment decisions they make.**

But separate research also shows that when women *do* invest their money, they can actually do better than men. Don't believe me? Well, look at the evidence of a company called DigitalLook. It tracked the portfolios of 10,000 investment clubs (where friends or workmates get together and invest relatively small amounts of money every month) in 2001, 2004 and 2005, and each time it found that women did better.

> *In their own words:*
>
> *'We have similar approaches to money, but my wife is more cautious when it comes to investing. I'm fairly cautious anyway, but I will invest in individual shares and I tend to make the decisions about investment funds.'*

As a woman you may be more risk averse, but taking some risk doesn't have to be a bad thing. In fact, when you do, you seem to manage pretty well. And for men, the message is that you may feel convinced your approach is the right one, but it could be because you feel more confident when you invest and not that you're necessarily better at making a profit.

Where will the money come from?

If you're going to save money for a long-term goal, you should start as soon as you can. You may feel like there's never any money left over, but if you've taken on board the budgeting advice in Chapter 4, you'll be able to draw up a new money plan and see whether you can cut back so you can 'create' some money for your savings pot.

Choosing your investment strategy

There are two ways that you can decide what you're going to do with your money and how you're going to make it grow:

1. Do-it-yourself

2. Using professional help.

Do-it-yourself

If you feel at home doing all your research by searching the internet, watching TV and reading the personal finance sections of the papers, you may be happy to be your own financial adviser.

Advantages

- You feel in direct control of every decision you make.
- You can make your decisions exactly when you want to.
- You won't have to pay for advice.
- You won't be exposed to any 'hard sell'.

Disadvantages

- If you're using the internet for research, you may suffer from information overload and potentially inaccurate information.

- There will be no-one to put the information into context.

- You will have to rely on your own financial expertise.

- You'll miss out on the chance of face-to-face advice.

The DIY approach is not something I'd recommend for any but the most straightforward decisions because I think most of us don't have the time or expertise to make the best financial choices. However, if you feel you'd like to make the decisions on your own, there are some web sites and publications that could be a useful starting point. I've mentioned a few price comparison web sites already that are good for getting details on competitive savings accounts and cash ISAs.

Moneyfacts (www.moneyfacts.co.uk) has a whole section devoted to savings best buys on its web site, as do other comparison services such as moneysupermarket.com and moneynet (www.moneynet.co.uk). Just be aware that you may get different answers from each site.

If you prefer, you can use the Financial Services Authority's own comparative tables (they're not called 'best buy' tables because the FSA doesn't rank the results). They're on www.moneymadeclear. fsa.gov.uk

When it comes to getting information about investments, the options are a bit trickier. The FSA tables cover investments such as pensions and ISAs that invest in share-based funds, but don't include information on past performance, only on how much you would pay in costs and charges.

Sites that do tell you about past performance include Trustnet (www.trustnet.co.uk) and Morningstar (www.morningstar.co.uk); and the Financial Times (www.ft.com) where you need to click on the 'managed funds' icon on the left-hand side of the home page. Past performance isn't a guide to the future (as they say on the adverts), but it can help you weed out the real turkeys.

Getting professional advice

If you don't feel confident in your financial expertise, you may prefer to use a professional financial adviser. Many people baulk at the idea, because financial advisers acquired a pretty awful reputation for the mis-selling that went on in the 1980s and 1990s (when it seemed half of them were mis-selling endowment mortgages and the rest were mis-selling pensions).

However, the industry has cleaned itself up since then, partly through some of its own initiatives but also because it's been forced to by the Financial Services Authority.

The benefit of using a financial adviser is that they should have a level of expertise you don't possess. However, it's not always easy to find a good financial adviser as while they do exist, so do the mediocre ones.

Advantages of an adviser (and not a glorified salesperson)

A professional adviser should have detailed research at their fingertips that you would not necessarily have access to.

A professional adviser can take a 'holistic' approach to your finances and can look at how one financial decision will affect others you've made or may make in the future.

A professional adviser should give you extra information that should make a real difference to your financial situation. For example, how to invest money in the most tax-efficient way.

And the disadvantages

You have to pay for the advice, although this disadvantage is not actually as clear cut as it might appear. There are many products that are no cheaper if you go direct to the company than if you use a financial adviser. Depending on the type of adviser you see, you may end up paying for your advice upfront by handing over a cheque or by having the money taken out of your premiums through commission.

You may not know whether your adviser is up to the job until it's too late. This is a familiar dilemma for many of us, although it doesn't just apply to financial advisers (plumbers, builders and car mechanics also spring to mind).

> How to make your financial decisions is as important as what you do with your money. In an ideal world, you and your partner would agree a way forward, but if the pros and cons listed above don't help, then maybe a list of your own 'benefits of going it alone' versus 'benefits of using a professional' would do the trick.

You might both feel happy making some financial decisions on your own (such as choosing a cash ISA for example, where the choice is relatively straightforward), but feel you'd rather leave the big decisions (such as what to do about a pension or where to invest so you have money for your children's education) to a professional. It doesn't have to be an either/or situation.

> If you want to buy products direct and know what you want, use a discount (or execution-only) broker to get some of the commission rebated. Ones to try include Bestinvest (www.bestinvest.co.uk) and Chartwell (www.chartwell.co.uk).

There are advisers ... and advisers

You may feel that the financial world is unnecessarily complicated and in many ways I'd have to agree with you. The different types of financial adviser that are allowed to give advice illustrate the point neatly.

The regulator, the FSA, turned the system of financial advice on its head a few years ago and is planning to make other significant changes in the near future, although these are still in the consultation phase and may change again. Any changes wouldn't come into force until 2009 at the absolute earliest.

So, bearing in mind the system is in a state of flux, I'll explain what the situation is at the moment and what you should be looking out for if you're going to use a financial adviser. I'll also point out how the advisers could change in the future.

The current system

There are three types of financial adviser, although only one of them is independent:

- tied
- multi-tied
- independent.

Tied

The clue's in the name here. A tied adviser is tied to one company, so can only sell you a product that's provided by that company. If someone else sells something much better, they're not allowed to tell you about it – by law.

There are several disadvantages to using a tied adviser. Importantly, many will be on a relatively small salary and a large commission, so they have to sell you something if they're going to pay their own bills.

It's a bit like hiring a personal shopper to get you the best outfit or gadget when they can buy from only one brand in the high street, and you've only got their word about how good the shop is.

Multi-tied

This is a kind of halfway house between tied advisers and those who are independent. A multi-tied adviser is allowed to recommend products from a range of financial providers that their company has linked up with. Again, these advisers are often on a small salary and large commission.

Many of the high street banks have linked up with specialist investment and pension companies – often because their own products were known to offer pretty poor value.

Using the personal shopper analogy, here your personal shopper would be able to go to one high street shop for clothes, one for shoes, one for furniture and so on. You'd have more choice than before, but it would still be pretty limited.

Independent

If you go to an independent financial adviser (IFA), you *should* get the best deal every time. That's because IFAs have no restrictions on the products they recommend. They can choose whichever policy they think matches your circumstances from the whole financial services 'market'. So here the personal shopper would be able to choose on your behalf from any shop they wanted to.

How are IFAs paid?

IFAs can be paid by fee or commission but must offer both options.

Fee basis

An IFA can charge you an upfront fee, which will probably be around £150 an hour on average (although more in London) depending on where you live, how experienced the IFA is and how large the firm is that they work for.

Some advisers are fee-based (i.e. they keep timesheets and charge an hourly rate), but cover the cost of the fee by taking a commission and rebating the 'unused' commission to you. You won't receive a cheque for the difference, as it will be paid back into the investment plan.

Commission basis

If you prefer, you can pay by commission. This means the money comes straight from your premiums. You don't have the pain of handing over money at the time, but it could end up costing you more in the long term. And as commission levels vary across different products and providers, you may not be sure whether the level of commission is a factor in their recommendation.

A word of caution

The creation of multi-tied advisers effectively increased the competition in the IFA sector. It meant that some IFAs decided they would concentrate on the wealthiest part of the market (those people who had tens or even hundreds of thousands of pounds they wanted to invest). So there are now fewer IFAs who are prepared to give advice to people who don't have tens of thousands of pounds to invest.

Finding an IFA

Recommendation from someone you know is always the best way, especially if your circumstances are broadly similar. But if you don't know where to start, the easiest way to find an independent financial adviser is to go to the IFA Promotions web site (www. unbiased.co.uk). IFA Promotions exists to promote the benefits of using independent advisers, so expect a bit of a sales message about how good they are.

If you want to make sure that the IFA is registered and is therefore legally allowed to give financial advice, you should look at the FSA's web site (http://www.moneymadeclear.fsa.gov.uk/tools/ check_our_register.html).

Qualifications to manage your money

At present an IFA (or in fact any financial adviser) only has to take a Certificate of Financial Planning (or an equivalent) exam to call themselves an adviser. There are some exceptions where the adviser has to have passed additional exams if they advise on areas such as lifetime mortgages (otherwise known as equity release) and long-term care.

If you want to make sure you're seeing someone who has a better understanding of some of the more complicated areas of money management, a good starting point might be someone who's passed more advanced exams. Qualifications to look out for include AFPC (Advanced Financial Planning Certificate) or someone who has CFP (Certified Financial Planner) status, which is *not* the same as a Certificate in Financial Planning.

What might change?

The FSA is currently looking at changing the rules and, at this stage, is proposing to create two tiers of adviser: 'professional financial planners' and 'general financial advisers'. There would also be the introduction of a basic level of advice called 'primary advice'.

Currently there's a debate about whether the changes should mean that advisers who are well qualified and charge a fee can call themselves independent, whether or not they sell products from the whole of the market. If that happens I think it will leave everyone completely baffled.

How do I know which adviser I'm seeing?

Advisers have to give you information, as soon as you have your first appointment or when they write to you, which explains what they do and whether they are tied, multi-tied or independent. It will also tell you how you can pay for the advice you receive.

How to get the best from your adviser

Knowing that the adviser is up to the job is only part of the picture. You don't use a financial adviser to be sold something, you use them for their expertise. That means they have to listen – and I mean really listen – to what you say. If the adviser is at all evasive about the following questions, don't reward them by becoming a client.

- **What is your background? (They should give you a potted career history.)**

- **What type of clients do you look after?**

- **How many clients do you have? (If it's a large number they may be more interested in new business than keeping existing clients happy.)**

- **How do you prefer to be paid?**

The next step

Once you've found a financial adviser you're happy with (or once you've decided to do the research yourself), you can start working out how you want to invest your money.

There are two main factors you have to take into account:

1. **How long you can leave your money invested for.**

2. **How much risk you are prepared to take.**

How long can you leave your money invested for?

This is fairly easy to work out. You either need access to the money in the near future, or you can afford to lock it away for a period of time. The longer you can lock it away, the more options you'll have available.

The financial industry is very fond of jargon like short, medium and long term, but less fond of spelling out exactly what these terms mean. It's generally accepted that anything less than five years counts as short term. That means there's no point in going anywhere near the stock market with your cash because you could lose money instead of making it.

But what is longer term? The fund management company Fidelity carried out detailed research over a 20-year period (from February 1987 to February 2007) and compared over 120 different ten-year periods within that time. It found that in 100 per cent of cases, people who invested both in UK-only share-based funds and a mix of UK and overseas share-based funds made money over a ten-year period. But over five years only 81 per cent of UK investors and 77 per cent of people who invested in international shares were in profit.

It's all about risk

I would say that risk is the most important factor when it comes to deciding how you are going to grow your wealth and yet that too is often talked about in terms that only the financial services industry understands.

Advisers often talk about 'cautious', 'balanced' or 'adventurous' investors, but I'm not convinced any of those terms explain how I feel about handing my money over to a particular company at any one time. On top of that, many of us feel differently about risk at different times in our lives and depending on what we're going to invest the money for. You probably wouldn't want to take a risk that your mortgage wouldn't be paid off, but you might be happy to take a risk if you'd received a large windfall that you weren't expecting.

> *In their own words:*
>
> *'I'm not very good at thinking about the technicalities of how I should be saving or investing my money. I almost have an allergy to talking about it! My partner had endless ideas about what I should be doing with my money and this caused lots of rows.'*

How much risk to take

The only way you can really find out what your attitude to risk is, is to ask yourself how you feel about the idea of your money going up and down in value. While you should invest for the 'long term', it's no good having sleepless nights while your money is invested. If you invest in shares, you can't expect steady upward growth with no dips (or even some hard falls). The key is to keep your eye on the horizon and not to let the ups and downs get in the way of long-term plans.

But don't feel it's an 'either/or' situation. If you can spare £100 a month from your income, you could split that so you pay £50 a month into an investment plan and £50 into savings (or £75/£25, whatever you feel comfortable with). It's another way of reducing your risk, as is drip-feeding your money throughout the year rather than paying in one lump sum.

By asking these types of questions, you and your partner will be able to create a picture of the amount of risk you really feel comfortable with. It's important that this is something you can agree on between you if it's joint money that's being invested.

> If you can't agree on a joint risk profile, then you could invest on the basis of each of your individual attitudes to risk.

Flexibility

I said that risk and how long you can leave your money locked away for would influence your investment decision, but it's also about how flexible the products are that you're advised to put your money into. If you have money locked into a product with a fixed term that wallops on hefty penalties if you have the cheek to change your plans, your options will be much more limited than if you had put your money into something that let you change the amount you invest, stop contributions altogether, switch to a different provider or cash it in without penalty.

Investment options

There are dozens of different types of investment product and I don't have space to explain the pros and cons of each of them here. What I'll do instead is describe some of the most popular financial products that you're likely to hear or read about (even if you haven't invested in one).

Equity ISAs

As mentioned earlier, the financial services industry is littered with jargon, and lots of words it uses are interchangeable. Here's one: *equity*. In this context, it simply means 'shares'. It means something different if you're talking about property when it refers to the value of your home over and above what you owe on your mortgage.

The reason I've started off with equity (or shares) ISAs is that they're the most popular form of stock market investment. They're particularly popular with women who like their flexibility. You can start an ISA one year and not pay into it the following year, cash it in without hefty penalties and, while there are charges to pay, they're not nearly as high as with some investment products.

> Every year you can put up to £7000 into an equity ISA and when you cash it in, you won't have to pay income or capital gains tax. These annual limits have stayed the same for years, but they will increase in 2008 by £200 to £7200.

There are several different types of equity ISA, but the most popular (by a long way) are those offered by mainstream fund management companies, which spread your money between a number of different shares (normally between 50 and 100).

There are hundreds of different companies offering equity ISAs; some of them are household names, others are well known in their field of expertise, but you may not have come across them if you've never invested in a share-based fund before. Don't worry about that because it's fairly easy to find out what their track record is. You or your financial adviser can research what kind of return they've generated over a period of one, two, five and ten years and whether that's better or worse than the average return. (You can use some of the web sites like Trustnet and Morningstar which I mentioned earlier.)

> You can't assume that a star performer one year will perform as well the next year, but one that's been consistently good has a better chance of doing well than one that's been consistently bad. But costs and charges are also important: the more money that's taken in charges, the lower the return you'll be left with.

Share-based funds are a good idea if you don't want to spend the time researching individual companies, because normally a professional fund manager does it for you. However, some equity ISAs spread your money through different companies simply by investing in those that make up one of the stock market indices (such as the FTSE 100 or FTSE All-Share).

So an equity ISA tracking the FTSE 100 would buy shares in companies that make up that index; and normally they'd be weighted to reflect the size of the company in relation to the others. In this case there's little or no management involved. They're less risky than funds that are managed by a professional in that you won't put your money into a fund that's run by someone who couldn't manage their way out of a paper bag. Costs and charges on tracker funds are also generally lower. The downside is that you don't get access to such a diversity of companies and that increases your risk.

Unit trusts, investment trusts and OEICS
If you put money into an equity ISA, what you'll actually be investing in is a unit trust, an investment trust or an OEIC. The 'ISA' just means there's no capital gains tax to pay on the proceeds when you cash it in.

I know there are a lot of different terms here, but there is a connection between them. Unit trusts, investment trusts and OEICs (which stands for open-ended investment companies) are simply funds that buy shares in a lot of companies. Investors can then buy a tiny (or larger) slice of the fund.

The difference between the three is down to the way the investment is structured. It's important because it affects how much you pay for the products and how much risk you're taking on. It's a bit too detailed to go into here, but you should know that there is a difference before you part with your money.

Shares

You may own some shares that you've bought or been given when a building society or financial company floated on the stock market. You don't have to put your money into share funds to invest in an equity ISA. You can simply buy shares in one company and hold them within the tax-efficient ISA wrapper (or you can transfer shares you already own, such as windfall or privatization shares).

Reducing risk

In order to get the most from money you're investing, you need to spread it around. Normally, whenever there's a newspaper article, TV or radio programme on this subject, someone wisely concludes that you shouldn't put 'all your eggs in one basket'. What that means is you've got to get the asset allocation right. Asset allocation simply means reducing your risk by spreading your money through different assets such as shares, cash, property and bonds.

Bonds

A bond is a really straightforward concept; it's just an IOU on a loan to a company or a government. It's like having a savings account in that you get interest on the money you've lent. The difference with a bond is that there's a chance you may not get back the money you loaned in the first place.

If you lend money to the UK government, the bond is called a gilt; if it's to a company, it's called a corporate bond. The rate of interest you receive on your bond depends on how risky the government or company is that you're lending your money to.

> You can put money into a corporate bond fund (a collection of different corporate bonds under one umbrella) and get the tax benefits of an ISA. But even though you're not actually investing in shares, corporate bond ISAs are sometimes referred to as 'equity' ISAs.

Property

This doesn't really need any explanation, does it? You either own a property or you don't. Except that you might own a bit of property through a fund. These work in the same way as share-based funds, except they buy a variety of commercial developments (to spread the risk) and let investors buy into the fund. Many experts view these as something you should put only a relatively low percentage of your money into.

Don't forget your pension

You shouldn't ignore your retirement, even if you're still feeling very young and frisky and it seems like a world away. You may not retire for 20 or 30 years, but you need a long time to build up enough to live on.

In 2007, the average pension fund was worth £29,000, according to pension and insurance company Legal and General.

That's not an annual figure, that's how much the entire fund was worth and that would buy an income of around £2000 a year. On average, people who retired had 1.4 pension pots, but that still meant they were getting an income of only £2900 a year or £56 a week. Not enough to retire in style.

It's not a pension, but retirement investing!

The difference between putting money into a pension and investing for your retirement is an important one. A pension is a particular kind of scheme or policy where you get a bit of a tax handout from the government in exchange for locking your money away until you retire and (in certain cases) converting the bulk of it into an annuity, which is a policy that pays out an income for the rest of your life.

Investing for your retirement is exactly that: using whatever investments suit you to build up some money. It could be a pension, but it does not have to be. What's important is that you find a method of squirrelling away enough money to see both of you through your well-earned retirement.

The real benefit of pensions is the fact they get tax relief, which essentially means 'free money from the government'. The disadvantage is that you can't get at the money before you reach a certain age so pensions aren't very flexible.

'Tax relief' doesn't really explain what the government contributes to your pension, so I'll spell it out:

- If you pay tax at the basic rate (currently 22 per cent, although it goes down to 20 per cent in 2008) and you want to pay £100 a month into your pension, you can do so by handing over just £78 a month to the pension company. The government adds the other £22 (that's the tax relief), so the amount that's actually invested is £100.

- If you're a higher rate taxpayer you get tax relief at 40 per cent. If you have an occupational pension it is added straightaway, but with a personal pension you have to claim the difference between basic and 40 per cent tax through your self-assessment tax return.

Reviewing what you have already

It's quite likely that you'll already have some money invested in one or more pensions. What you have to make sure is that you're both well provided for in retirement. Statistics show that women retire on less than men, sometimes a lot less. And while they invest less, they live for longer, so a woman with a pension fund of £100,000 would be able to convert that into an income of only around £6300 a year, whereas a man who'd saved the same amount could get £6600 a year.

Different types of pension scheme

Today, most employers have to offer a pension scheme. Those with five or more workers have to have a stakeholder pension, but it doesn't mean that paying into one will make you rich when you retire. That's because the employer doesn't have to contribute a penny to it, whereas with most other employer pension schemes, they do.

All they have to do is set one up and make it relatively easy for you to pay into it. However, employers that do contribute typically match scheme members' payments pound for pound up to a limit of 5 per cent of their salary.

If your employer doesn't have a stakeholder pension, there are several other types it may operate. For example:

A final salary pension scheme: This does what it says on the tin. Your pension is based on the salary you earn at retirement (often an average of the last three years). Normally you earn 1/80th or 1/60th of your salary for every year you're a member of the scheme. Your pension isn't directly affected by the ups and downs of the stock market, because the employer can't just chop and change what they pay as a pension whenever they feel like it. But these schemes are not risk-free. If your employer goes bust or the pension scheme is wound up, you may get only a percentage of the pension you're entitled to.

Money purchase pension: Money purchase schemes have become much more popular over recent years, as employers have realized just how expensive it is to provide their workers with a guaranteed pension at retirement. Here the risk falls on you and not your employer. What your employer agrees to do is to pay into a fund on your behalf but the money you get at retirement will depend on how much has been paid in and how well the fund has performed, not on your salary or how long you've been a member of the scheme.

Group personal pension (GPP) scheme: This is similar to the stakeholder pension example above, and as with the stakeholder pension, the employer doesn't have to pay a penny into it on your behalf. Unlike a money purchase scheme, you can take a GPP with you when you leave the company.

Around 400,000 GPP and stakeholder schemes exist with no contribution from the employer. If your employer doesn't pay into its pension scheme, you may be better off choosing one of your own. The only real advantage to joining your employer's stakeholder or GPP scheme is that money you pay in will be taken straight from your salary before you can spend it.

A richer life together

Once you know what you want your money to help you do, you can start putting the plans in place so that you get there. What I hope this chapter has given you is an understanding of the different types of financial advice available, an insight into why it's so important that you understand how you feel about risk and – above all – the confidence to take the steps towards a wealthier future together.

CHAPTER 7

When two becomes three…

It's often said that if parents stopped to work out the cost of having a child before the event they'd never take the plunge. Thankfully few couples get out the spreadsheets, or if they do, they generally keep quiet about it.

And once you have children, you have much better things to do with your time than add up the costs, but over the years a number of banks and financial companies have attempted to do just that. The figures vary widely but they're generally pretty scary; add in the cost of private education and, frankly, you're into the realms of telephone-number figures.

Not surprisingly you can't become a parent without making financial sacrifices, either by cutting back on what you spend, working longer hours than you want to or staying in a job that you'd rather not do because the salary is good. If you've *planned* your family, you should at least have had some time to prepare, but if your baby is a happy accident, you won't even have that luxury.

One thing that's certain is the more information you have, the better placed you will be to take the right decisions. This chapter isn't designed to be a comprehensive guide to all that goes with parenthood, but it will give you some valuable pointers about the financial implications of having a family.

> While the financial impact is important, there will be a massive emotional one as well. I don't just mean how each of you may feel about impending parenthood, but how the adjustments you have to make as a consequence may change your status within the relationship and what effect that may have on how you deal with money.

Preparing for the new arrival

It doesn't matter how many self-help books you read, you won't really know what the arrival of a baby will mean until it happens. What you may be surprised by is how your perception of yourself changes. Many parents say they find it easier to make responsible decisions about their lifestyle and budget than they ever did before.

> If your mortgage deal is due to run out, you may want to remortgage as soon as you can. Remortgaging can be an issue if you're on maternity pay, and if the lender works on the basis of affordability, childcare costs can be taken off your income before it works out how much it will lend.
>
> Alternatively you may want to make reduced mortgage payments (or take a payment holiday), although unpaid interest will be added to the loan.

Your income may be reduced by 25 per cent or more if you take maternity leave, at a time when you have a whole new list of things to buy. Don't underestimate how you or your partner will feel (depending on who's reading this) about the fact that they won't be earning while they're looking after the baby.

> *In their own words:*
>
> *'We decided that when we had a baby I'd give up work, but it's difficult being a "kept woman" after being used to my own money. I don't really get any control and that's a new experience.'*

According to Relate counsellors, having a baby can be a time when conflicts over money are easily triggered.

- If you're on maternity leave or are staying at home to look after your baby, it's not unusual for you to think your partner should take a different job: one that either pays more or that gives them more time to help at home.

- Conversely, if your partner tries to earn more by doing overtime, you may feel annoyed that he's never there.

If the idea of not having your own money is really causing a problem, talk about it. But before you do, work out whether it's the fact you don't have any of your own money for treats (either for yourself or a present for your partner), or that you're reliant on your partner financially. The solution may be as easy as having a small amount of your "own" money each week or month to spend as you wish.

Great financial expectations

If you're working, your employer should be able to cushion the financial blow. Some are more generous than others but, as a guide, this is what you will be entitled to:

- maternity leave
- maternity pay
- paternity leave and pay.

Maternity leave

If you're pregnant and you're employed then you're entitled to take a year's maternity leave. It's as simple as that – and you are still entitled to maternity leave even if you are in your probationary period. Although you can take a whole year off, your leave is actually made up of two parts: *ordinary maternity leave*, during which time your work contract continues and you receive all the benefits of being employed except your wages (such as a car allowance and gym membership, etc.), and *additional maternity leave* where your contract continues but you won't necessarily receive all the benefits.

An employer cannot discriminate against you because you've taken maternity leave, but many women claim that their career stalls or its progression slows once they return to work.

In their own words:

'I was worried that I'd lose out by taking maternity leave and that's exactly what happened. I was running a department, but my employer promoted the person covering my maternity leave and now she's my boss. It's made work very difficult.'

Although you automatically qualify for maternity leave, you must tell your employer about your pregnancy by the 15th week before the baby is due in order to get it. You'd be around 25 weeks pregnant at this stage so it would probably be quite difficult to hide the fact you're pregnant anyway.

> If you can afford to carry on paying into your employer's pension scheme while you're on paid maternity leave, you should do so. Your own contributions will be based on your lower maternity pay, but your employer's will be based on your full pay. It's more money from your boss…for free!

Maternity pay

You qualify for statutory maternity pay if you were working for your employer before you became pregnant and you earn at least an average of £87 a week (2007–08). You'll receive 90 per cent of your average pay in the first 6 weeks and a flat rate (currently £112.75 a week) for the other 33 weeks, although some employers pay more than the statutory minimum.

In their own words:

'I had six weeks' maternity pay at 90 per cent of my salary, then the next four and a half months at a third of my salary, and then the statutory rate. It meant we had time to get used to the idea of less money.'

Maternity allowance

If you don't qualify for maternity pay because you don't earn enough or because you work for yourself, you should be able to claim maternity allowance for 39 weeks at either £112.75 a week (tax year 2007–08) or 90 per cent of your average earnings, whichever is lower. You have to pass an 'employment test', which basically means you have to have been employed or working for yourself for a minimum of 26 weeks out of 66 weeks before the week your baby is due.

Paternity leave

Fathers are also allowed to take up to two weeks off and receive paternity pay. However, not everyone qualifies: only workers who've been employed for 26 weeks at the 15th week before the baby is due. (So you must have started working for the company approximately a week before your wife or partner became pregnant.)

What will you have to buy?

According to the parenting web site Raising Kids (www.raisingkids. co.uk) you'll need to spend almost £700 just to get your baby through the first few weeks. Of course, you can bring down the cost by borrowing from friends and family but, unless you're very lucky, there's almost certainly something you'll have to buy from new.

Don't underestimate how the emotional side of things will affect your decision. It's a bit like spending on a wedding. You may feel pushed into buying 'the best' (i.e. the priciest) because you don't want to cut corners.

 Write a shopping list of 'must-haves' and 'nice to haves'. Look at the specialist parenting web sites (Raising Kids, as above, or www.ukparentslounge.com), as well as shopping comparison sites (e.g. www.pricerunner.co.uk or www.kelkoo.co.uk) and consumer advice sites like Which? (www.which.co.uk).

- Buy things you need from charity shops, eBay, or get them for free from the recycling network freecycle (www.freecycle.org). Supermarkets are a great place to shop for baby and children's clothes.

- Take advantage of baby clubs to get vouchers on everything from nappies to toothpaste for kids. Boots and Tesco are two retailers with baby clubs that you can sign up to online. You can also register with nappy manufacturers for money-off vouchers.

Losing one salary

In an ideal world, if you've planned to have a family, you'd use the time when you were both earning to build up some savings, but that's not always possible. However, what you must try to do is pay off any debts, or at least repay as much as you can so you know the payments will be affordable when your income shrinks.

If you owe money on credit cards, swap them to a 0 per cent deal (but watch out for the balance transfer fees). If you can afford to pay off loans early, contact your bank or the loan provider and find out whether there's a penalty for doing so.

It's back to the budget

Hopefully you'll have kept on top of your budgeting, but if you've allowed things to lapse, now's the time to get back in control.

In their own words:

'We knew we had to make cutbacks, but because we spent less money on going out it was quite easy. I think we were both surprised at how "grown up" we could be.'

Consolidating your loans

If you think your borrowing has got out of hand, you may need to consider drawing up a repayment agreement (you'll find details in Chapter 2). In general terms it's not a good idea to borrow more to pay off existing debts. However, it may make sense to convert credit card debt into a personal loan, if you can get one at a low interest rate and if you can't get a 0 per cent balance transfer deal on your cards.

Be very wary about borrowing more against the value of your house to pay off your credit cards. You'll be converting unsecured debt into secured debt. What that means is that you could risk losing your home. Debts like credit cards and personal loans are not secured against your home, so if you can't pay back the money, creditors can't repossess your home. But if you consolidate your loan and secure it on your home, the lender may repossess it if you can't keep up the repayments.

Money for nothing

You're entitled to child benefit, money to pay into a child trust fund and possibly child tax credit as well.

Child benefit

You can't apply for child benefit until you've registered your baby's birth and have a birth certificate. Depending on where you live, there may be a long wait for an appointment to register your baby.

You should have a child benefit claim form in the 'bounty pack' (which contains things like baby wipes, disinfectant and shampoo) that you'll be given when your baby is born, otherwise you can download one from the Revenue and Customs web site (http://www.hmrc.gov.uk/childbenefit/claim-info.htm). In tax year

WHEN TWO BECOMES THREE...

2007–08 child benefit is paid at the rate of £18.10 a week for the first child and £12.10 a week for each child after that.

Child trust fund

Once you start claiming child benefit, you'll automatically be issued with a child trust fund (CTF) information pack, followed by a voucher for £250 from the government (£500 for families on a low income). You've got a year to decide where you're going to invest the money, otherwise the government invests it for you. Lots of parents have complained that they've found the information hard to understand and have felt baffled by the choices on offer.

The problem is that it's difficult to get advice about what to do with your child trust fund. Independent financial advisers don't want to know – because the amounts are so small (you can only save up to £1200 a year) it's not really worth their while.

The child trust fund web site (www.childtrustfund.gov.uk) does talk through all the options, but it can't really point you in the right direction.

I understand that it's tempting to ignore the CTF information that comes through the letterbox. Let's face it, you'll have far more important things on your mind, but it is free money your child is being given. If you don't choose a financial provider your child won't lose out entirely, but you (or rather they) could miss out on up to a year's interest and you won't have control over which company runs the CTF for your child.

In their own words:

'Don't worry too much about whether you've picked the right fund. Open one as soon as you can – as we did – and pay in as much as you can afford.'

Child tax credit

If you've not claimed a tax credit before, you'll have missed out on this peculiarly complex form of state assistance. If you have children and earn less than £58,175 (in tax year 2007–08) or £66,350 if it's the first year of your child's life, you should be eligible (some believe you should fill in the form even if your income is higher, to get 'in the system'). That's the good news. The bad news is that you'll then enter the labyrinth that is the claims process.

In theory it should be a helpful benefit: child tax credit (CTC) is paid to the main carer – normally the mother. It doesn't matter whether you work or not, you're still entitled to it and you can be fairly well off as a household and still qualify for some help.

The problem is that the calculation about how much CTC you may receive is so complicated that many of the staff who deal with the claims don't seem to understand the rules.

If you do put in a claim, my advice is not to assume that whatever you get paid is yours to keep. Basically, the amount you receive is provisional, which means if your circumstances change you'll probably have to pay some of it back. In some cases, couples have been told they have to pay back thousands of pounds.

There have been some improvements to the backlog of cases, but the problem has certainly not gone away. I've just Googled 'child tax credits' and 'confusion' and spent a few minutes wading through the results. Time after time parents said they had to repay child tax credits when they had already queried the amount they were receiving and been told it was correct.

In their own words:

'We looked at applying for child tax credit, but decided not to as I was worried I'd have to repay it at some stage if there was a mistake. I wasn't sure whether we'd qualify anyway as it was so complicated to work out.'

I'd still advise you to apply, but you must keep on top of your claim, inform Revenue and Customs if your circumstances change and be prepared to be as tenacious as a terrier when you're following it up. Do also keep a record of what you've sent them, what you've said and what you've been told, in case there's a dispute further down the line.

Childcare costs

If you want to go back to work, or you have to because you can't manage on one salary, you might be able to get help with childcare costs. There are two sources: your employer through childcare vouchers and the state through the childcare element of the working tax credit (which is means-tested). You are entitled to claim only one or the other, not both, for the same costs.

If you want more information about finding childcare and how to pay for it, look at the Daycare Trust web site (www.daycaretrust.org.uk). Your local authority will have its own Children's Information Service (CIS), which includes information on all registered childcare schemes for your area. There's no national CIS web site, so it's a case of looking at your local council's site and doing a search on 'children's information service' within that.

An alternative way to the same information is to go to the government web site ChildcareLink (www.childcarelink.gov.uk), which is comprehensive and easy to navigate.

Employee childcare vouchers

From 2005 employers have been able to provide their workers with childcare vouchers that are worth up to £55 a week and are free of tax and national insurance (NI). Some employers offer vouchers through a 'salary sacrifice' scheme. It means you lose some salary to pay for them. It looks like you're just paying £55 for £55 vouchers, but you pay out of gross salary (before tax and NI have been taken off), so if you're a basic rate taxpayer, the £55 of vouchers actually cost you only £37 (at 2007–08 tax rates).

The £55 a week is per parent and not per child, so if both of you work and each of your employers offers the childcare voucher scheme, you're both able to benefit from it. You must use your vouchers to pay for registered childcare (so they can't be paid to grandparents, for example, who may babysit as a favour).

Childcare element of working tax credit

You may be able to claim up to 80 per cent of your childcare costs up to a maximum of £175 a week for one child and £300 a week if you've got two or more children (so the actual amount of money you'd receive would be a maximum of £140 and £240 respectively). As with childcare vouchers, you have to use registered childcare.

CHAPTER 8

Protecting what you both have

Thinking about how you can protect your financial security in the event of serious illness – or worse – is not the most cheerful of subjects. But if you have any joint financial commitments (such as a mortgage) it's something you should consider and if you have children, it's absolutely vital.

There are all kinds of different insurance policies on the market, but the difficulty a lot of us have is trying to work out which may be useful, and which will do more for the salesperson than they ever will for us. You'll probably have heard about some of the different ways you can protect yourself against disaster striking. They include:

- **life insurance**
- **income protection**
- **critical illness cover**
- **private medical insurance.**

How much you spend and what you insure against will largely come down to how cautious you are and your budget.

Employee benefits

If you're employed, your first step is to find out what your company offers through its website or human resources department. Most people don't bother to check what's on offer but it could save you a lot of money. Many employers have free life insurance (it's called 'death in service benefit', but it amounts to the same thing), some will provide income protection and others will go much further and have all kinds of insurance that could cost you thousands of pounds a year if you bought them privately.

Death in service benefit limits

Companies tend to offer two, four or ten times your salary as a death in service lump sum. That means if you die while you're still working for the company, what your spouse, civil partner or dependants will get will be based on your salary at the time (although bonuses and commission aren't usually included).

> There's obviously a huge advantage in getting your insurance cover through your employer because it's free or cheaper than if you bought it directly from an insurance company. You also won't have to go through an individual assessment – you'll automatically be covered if you're eligible under your employer's own rules – and companies can negotiate better benefits for their workers.
>
> The main disadvantage relates to what happens when you leave that employer. In some cases you may be able to take your policy with you to your new job but, if you can't, you might not be able to afford a replacement and the older you are, the more expensive this insurance is.

In their own words:

'I was never bothered about the extras my company offered until we got married, then I realized how valuable the benefits were.'

If you have to buy it yourself

If you don't have a generous company or you're self-employed and can't get covered by your partner's scheme, you'll have to bite the bullet and look at what you can afford for yourself.

There are two types of insurance that I think are important and others that will come down to what you can afford and how much cover you want.

Must-haves

The 'must-haves' are life insurance and income protection.

Life insurance

The cheap and cheerful route would be to take out enough life insurance to pay off the mortgage (or other debts) if one of you were to die before they've been cleared. Life insurance that lasts only for a specified number of years, rather than until you die, is called term assurance. It's normally set up for 25 years or whatever your mortgage term is and is much cheaper than 'whole of life' insurance for the simple reason that there's a fairly good chance you won't die in that period.

There are two types of term assurance:

- **decreasing term assurance**
- **level term assurance.**

Decreasing term assurance

For repayment mortgages the cheapest option is to take out 'decreasing term assurance'. It decreases as the outstanding mortgage goes down, although the premiums remain the same.

Level term assurance

If you have an interest-only mortgage, you should choose level term assurance and you can buy a straightforward policy that will last for 10, 20 or 25 years, or pay extra for one that's more flexible.

For example, a renewable term assurance policy is one that you can extend at the end of its term without having another medical, while convertible term assurance lets you convert your policy into one that lasts until you die, again without an additional medical.

> ### Single policies
>
> If you're covering a mortgage, the most obvious option would seem to be to take out a joint policy, but it's not necessarily the best one. If you have a joint policy and one of you dies, the other partner would be left without any cover of their own (because the policy only pays out once), whereas if you take out a single policy on each of your lives, you'll have life insurance in your own right – no matter what happens to the other partner.
>
> It may cost only 5–10 per cent more but it also means that if you were to get divorced, you could each take your policy with you (whereas you can't divide a joint life policy).

Write the policy in trust and save tax

You should also get your life insurance policy written in trust. The language sounds dusty and off-putting, but the principle behind it is very sound.

If you take out a life insurance policy in the usual way, the proceeds form part of your estate. Under the current rules anything you leave worth more than the IHT threshold (currently £300,000) could be subject to inheritance tax. Married couples and those in a civil partnership can transfer assets to each other free of IHT and can also increase their IHT threshold up to £600,000.

However, a large life insurance policy could still trigger an IHT bill for some. You can avoid that by writing it in trust, when the payout doesn't form part of your estate. The other advantage is that your heirs will not have to wait until probate has been granted before they receive the payout. Probate is simply a legal form that enables the executors of the will to carry out the person's wishes but it can take time.

Once you've got the mortgage covered, you need to sit down and work out exactly what each of you would have to pay for if the other one were to die, and how much of that you'd like to insure. Once you've done that, you can shop around for a quote.

The good news is that life insurance isn't expensive. In fact it's one financial product where prices have fallen sharply over the past decade and you'd probably be able to insure the average mortgage for the cost of a takeaway meal every month.

For example, according to specialist broker LifeSearch (www.

lifesearch.co.uk) a 29-year-old, non-smoking male could expect to pay around £9.60 a month for £150,000 of cover over a 25-year period (assuming that the amount insured remained at £150,000 and didn't decrease). A 29-year-old, non-smoking female would pay about £2 a month less at £7.85.

> Life insurance policies normally pay out a lump sum when the policyholder dies, but it can be cheaper to buy a 'family income benefit' policy that pays a monthly 'income'. Money is paid out tax-free and it can be a useful way of replacing your spouse's or partner's salary.

Income protection

This type of policy is designed to pay part of your salary if you can't work because you're ill. Typically you might insure 50–60 per cent of your salary before tax if you were buying a policy privately and up to 75 per cent if you took one out through your company. Payments are tax-free if you buy the policy privately, but taxed if paid through your employer, which is why the limits are different.

I think these policies are a good idea in principle and I've had one for a long time so I'm not just saying that, but not all are the same; indeed some of them have some pretty nasty catches.

The problem is that you may not recognize the catches for yourself, which is why I wouldn't recommend buying an income protection policy without taking expert advice. Here I'll try to point you in the right direction by giving you a couple of examples of how getting it right can make a huge difference to any payout.

Occupation rules

You might think that if you were ill and couldn't work, your income protection policy would pay out. Well, it might not. The financial services industry has honed its wriggling skills over many years and has come up with all kinds of cunning ways to avoid paying claims.

The most common relates to the work you're fit to do if you've been ill. Some companies will pay out if you can't do your own job (called 'own occupation'), some if you can't do your job *or* a similar one (called 'suited for occupation') and others only if you can't carry out a list of tasks. Typically there might be six tasks you're tested on and you'd have to be unable to do three of them for your claim to succeed.

This is where it gets a bit scary. You'd have to be pretty ill or incapacitated to be unable to complete the tasks you're assessed on. They include things like being able to use a pen, pencil or keyboard with either hand; the ability to lift a 1 kg weight and carry it for 5 metres; and the ability to answer a telephone and relay a message. Now I don't know about you, but I'm not quite sure what the point of a policy is if you must be unable to type a few words and carry a bag of sugar before it will pay out.

How your job affects your premiums
How old you are, whether you're male or female, and your state of health will determine how much you pay for income protection, but so will the job you do. There are normally four categories, with category 1 being the lowest risk (office work, for example) and 4 being the highest risk (such as heavy manual labour).

Guaranteed premiums
The other potential catch to look out for is what happens to your premiums. If you don't opt for something called 'guaranteed premiums' you could find the policy becomes unaffordable just at the moment when you need it most.

Premiums that aren't guaranteed can be revised by the

insurance company at any time. And they're very rarely revised downwards (it's a kind of flying pig moment if it happens). What's far more likely is that they are increased – sometimes quite significantly – every few years. Guaranteed premiums are more expensive initially but they can work out cheaper in the end.

> ### Index linking
>
> It's a good idea to have inbuilt indexation so that the amount of money you receive has a chance of keeping up with inflation (and therefore, hopefully, with your wages).

Deferred period

The deferred period is the time before the policy will pay out: the longer it is, the cheaper the policy. The shortest deferred period on offer is usually four weeks, although a few specialist providers offer 'day one cover', which is useful if you're self-employed with few savings, but *very* expensive.

The best thing to do is to try to tie it in with the sick pay package that your employer offers. If you're self-employed or your employer isn't particularly generous, you'll probably have to build up some savings to take you through the first few months. Six months is a typical deferred period and reducing that to 13 weeks will increase the premiums substantially; but increasing it to 52 weeks will cut the premiums by far less.

An income protection policy that will pay out £1000 a month to age 60, deferred for six months, would cost a 29-year-old, non-smoking male who worked as an office manager £11.10 a month, while a female in similar circumstances would pay £12.23. These premiums are a lot less than those usually quoted because unemployment cover hasn't been included.

It's up to you

Depending on your circumstances you may want to have critical illness cover and/or private medical insurance.

Critical illness cover

Critical illness insurance is supposed to pay out a cash sum if you're diagnosed with a serious or 'critical' illness. It's one of those policies that has its fans and critics in equal measure, but I don't think it's a must-have. One of the downsides is that it can be expensive. The other is that it can be quite difficult to work out exactly what the policy will cover you for. For example, some types of cancer and heart disease don't fall under the umbrella of being a critical illness.

It's often cheaper if you buy this cover as an add-on to life insurance that's linked to a mortgage, but it's still not that cheap. Using the earlier example, the £150,000 life insurance policy for a 29-year-old, non-smoking man that cost £9.60 would rise to £39.90 if critical illness insurance was included and from £7.85 to £39.97 for a woman of the same age.

Private medical insurance (PMI)

This can be a matter of principle or politics as much as one of hard cash. Some people don't like the idea of going private; others don't like the idea of NHS waiting lists or not having access to expensive drugs.

However, unless you can take out PMI through a subsidized scheme run by your employer, it can be costly. The cost rises the older you get and – more importantly – there's no guarantee that the cover you have one year will continue until the next.

When you buy medical insurance, you probably think of it as a long-term contract, but in fact it's an annual policy just like car insurance. That means the insurance company can change the terms and conditions at the end of each year. They can decide they won't cover certain illnesses or that they won't pay for certain drugs and if that happens there's not much you can do about it.

The application process

I'm devoting a bit of space to the application process because it's absolutely vital that you understand what's involved. If you don't you could find you pay into a policy that turns out to be worthless. It's also another warning about the importance of getting advice when you take out income protection, critical illness or private medical insurance.

Sometimes when you're sold these policies over the phone or internet, you may not realize how much information you have to provide on your application form. But you are expected to provide your *full* medical history. And by that, I mean details of just about everything that's ever happened to you (barring the occasional cough or cold).

Over the years I've reported on enough stories about people who've tried to make a claim for one illness only to have it turned down because they didn't tell the company about a seemingly entirely unrelated problem, to know that if you don't tell the insurer everything you could find your claim is turned down flat or that you get a reduced payout. It may not be logical, but it's the way the industry works.

> If you're in any doubt about whether to include some information about your medical history, include it. The insurance company will decide whether it's relevant or not. Don't take any notice of a salesperson who says you only have to tell the insurer about important or serious illnesses. They're wrong.

Leave well alone

Payment protection insurance

I talked about these policies in detail in Chapter 4, so I won't go over old ground here. If you really feel it's worth having, check the comparison sites I mentioned so you pay as little as possible.

Mortgage payment protection insurance (MPPI)

MPPI policies are designed to cover your mortgage payments if you can't work due to illness or because you've lost your job. Some experts think these policies are a good idea but I'm not a fan. If you're self-employed you could find it really difficult to claim under the unemployment clause anyway.

MPPI policies tend to have more exclusions than, say, income protection does, so you may not always be able to claim for back problems or stress (which make up a large percentage of claims on income protection policies). Also, the policies only pay out for 12 or 24 months, so if you're unable to return to work, you'd still have to find money to cover your mortgage once the policy stopped covering it.

Writing a will

Protecting what you've built up or earned over the years isn't just about taking out insurance policies, you should also write a will. I'm sure you realize it's something that you should do, but maybe you haven't got round to it yet. If that's your situation you're in good company because around two-thirds of adults haven't made one either. But just because most people haven't made a will, doesn't make it OK for you to do the same.

So why haven't you made a will? Is it because:

- you don't think you need one?
- it's too depressing to think about?
- you keep meaning to do it, but you haven't got the time?
- you don't know what you need to do?

They're all understandable reasons for sitting on your hands, but not for leaving your nearest and dearest trying to sort out a financial mess as well as cope with the emotional turmoil of losing you. I know that's harsh, but sadly it is the reality of what dying without a will could mean.

Let's look at those reasons one by one.

You don't think you need one

Well, actually you probably do. If you're married or in a civil partnership, the law does give your spouse or civil partner some rights, but it doesn't necessarily mean they will end up with everything if you were to die – or even with everything you'd hoped to leave them.

The limits on how much your spouse or civil partner would automatically inherit depend on whether you have children and where you live in the UK.

Married or civil partners

If you're living in England, Wales or Northern Ireland and are married or in a civil partnership but have no children, your spouse or civil partner would inherit the first £200,000 of what you've left, plus half the rest, while your parents (or brothers and sisters, or nephews and nieces) inherit the rest.

The only way your spouse or civil partner would get everything is if you don't have any children and there are no surviving parents or brothers and sisters either. Any property that's owned jointly as joint tenants also passes to the survivor. If you are married and have children your spouse or civil partner would inherit the first £125,000 and a life interest in half the rest. In Northern Ireland the 'life interest' element depends on the number of children.

In Scotland if you were married with no children, your spouse would inherit the first £300,000 of your estate plus what are called 'plenishings' – which basically means furniture from the house – worth up to £24,000 plus a further £75,000. The rest would go to your parents, to be split with brothers and sisters. Only if there were no surviving parents or brothers and sisters would the remainder of the estate pass to your spouse. If you have children, your spouse would inherit the first £300,000 plus furniture etc. worth up to £24,000 and a further £42,000. The rest would go to your children.

Living together
In England, Wales and Northern Ireland if you live together but aren't married and die without a will, your partner would inherit the house only if it was owned jointly and as joint tenants. If you had bought your property as tenants in common, your share of it would become part of your estate and if there was no will, it would go to your children (if you had any) or, if there were no children, your parents, or your brothers and sisters.

If you wanted to try to claim some of your partner's assets, you'd have to go to court. In England and Wales you'd apply under the Inheritance (Provision for Family and Dependants) Act 1975. In Scotland, it would be the Family Law Act, which gives the cohabiting partner the right to apply to court for either a lump sum payment or for property to be transferred out of the deceased partner's estate.

It's too depressing to think about

I understand this idea but once you've sorted it out you won't have to think about it again. You won't have that anxious feeling of 'I know I should do something about this' which can be a worry in itself. You'll know it's all been dealt with.

You keep meaning to do it

This one's simple: make the time. If necessary schedule it in your diary so you both sit down and draw up a list of what you have and who you'd like to leave it to. Once you've started the process, you'll probably find you're much more inspired to get your will sorted out and once it's sorted, you won't be wasting any more time thinking about what you should be doing.

You don't know what you need to do

There's lots of information on the internet about what's involved in drawing up a will. If you want non-commercial information, you could look at Citizens Advice 'adviceguide' pages (www.adviceguide.org.uk). Alternatively you could try the BBC web site – www.bbc.co.uk/parenting – and click on the 'family matters' icon.

If you've already got a will you may still need to get another one. For example, if it was drawn up before you got married or entered a civil partnership in England or Wales (but not Scotland), it will be invalid, unless you drew it up knowing you were going to get married and added a clause saying that the will should still be valid after the event.

Divorce does not revoke a will but will prevent money or assets from going to your ex-spouse or civil partner (but not to their children or other family members). As before, this does not apply to Scotland.

Appointing a guardian

If that's not enough to persuade you, there's another really compelling non-financial reason for making a will if you have children. And that's to appoint a guardian who'll look after them if you both die. It's all pretty grim stuff I know, but if you make a will at least you'll have control over who brings up your children. If you don't your children may end up living with someone whom you wouldn't have chosen as a guardian.

Saving tax

If you don't have children, there's one other reason that may persuade you – it could save you tax! If your estate is worth more than £300,000 (in the 2007–08 tax year) and you are not married or in a civil partnership, or over £600,000 if you are, your heirs could have to pay inheritance tax. A will can include a number of inheritance tax-saving measures, as well as spelling out who gets what. A good solicitor or financial adviser would be able to explain the options to you.

How to go about it

Once you've decided to make a will you've got three choices:

- **do-it-yourself**
- **use a will-writing company**
- **get a solicitor to do it for you.**

Doing it yourself is obviously the cheapest option, but it may not be the best. Many solicitors say they get a significant amount of their business untangling DIY wills. I don't know whether that's accurate or just designed to send us straight to the solicitor's offices, but what you decide to do will probably come down to how complex your affairs are (i.e. if you've got a few or many assets, and/or a simple or complicated family situation).

If you prefer to use a will-writer I'd just issue one word of warning: anyone can be one and they don't even need to have professional indemnity insurance. That doesn't mean you can't find a good one, but it's a bit of a lottery. I suggest that you look at someone who is a member of the Institute of Professional Willwriters (www.ipw.org.uk). Its members have to sit professional exams and have at least £2 million worth of insurance. They also have to take professional exams on a regular basis, are covered by a code of conduct and have to undergo a criminal records bureau (CRB) check.

Getting a will drawn up by a will-writer or solicitor doesn't have to be expensive. You would expect to pay £150–£250 for a straightforward 'mirror' will, which is often recommended for married couples with assets worth up to £600,000. More complex wills designed to minimise IHT liability can cost many hundreds of pounds.

If you want to use a solicitor, just make sure you use one who specializes in wills and probate. If you don't have any friends or family who can recommend a good solicitor, you can search for one on the Law Society web site (www.lawsociety.org.uk for England and Wales and www.lawscot.org.uk for Scotland).

In their own words:

'We put off drawing up a will for far too long because we didn't know who to ask to sort out our affairs. Once we decided on the executors it was all pretty straightforward.'

Appointing executors

You need to think carefully about who will act as your executors. Their job is to make sure the wishes expressed in your will are carried out properly.

You can appoint up to four executors who can also be beneficiaries of the will, but no-one who stands to gain from the will can witness you signing it. It's down to you who you appoint as executors; they can be family members or a solicitor or both.

The key is to think about the kind of job they'd do and how they'd find the process, and make sure that they are happy to take on the task before you name them in your will.

Thinking about what may happen if you die prematurely or become so ill that you cannot work for a period of time is difficult. However, if you follow the advice in this chapter you should be able to build up some protection according to what's on offer from your work, how much money you have and how much you want to spend. What you should be able to do is to understand the difference between a policy that should pay out when you need it and one where the insurer can hide behind the small print. And that information isn't just valuable, it could be priceless.

CHAPTER 9

Troubleshooting

One of the benefits of knowing what you want from your money and how much you have is that you spend far less time worrying about it.

If you don't know what's going on, you often fear the worst. But if you're back in the driving seat and know the truth (whether it's good or bad), you can at least plan your next move. And that's what this chapter is about. It will tell you how to make sure your plans are on track, and what to do if they've taken a bit of a detour.

Good financial habits are for life, but that doesn't mean that the money plan you drew up when you first moved in together or got married will work for you today. You may have different expectations about what you want from your money and how you hope to get there. On top of that, your own circumstances may have changed. It's a bit like trying to struggle into clothes that don't fit you any more. They don't feel good and rarely make you look your best.

Perhaps:

- You or your partner have changed jobs. It could mean you're earning a lot more or a lot less than you were a few years ago.

- You or your partner have given up work altogether. Maybe you planned to go back to work after having children and have changed your mind.

- You or your partner would like to start your own business.

- Your spending has been creeping up in a key area. You might have bought an expensive car, your mortgage deal might have come to an end or you might be spending more on going out and not realized just how much more.

- You might have got behind with your credit card or loan repayments.

Just as your relationship will have its ups and downs, so will your relationship with money. If you were on your own, it would be something you could deal with in your own way, but it's different when you're living with someone or are married. Even if you keep your money quite separate, what you choose to do with your cash is likely to affect your partner in some way.

If you start spending more money or indulging in secretive spending, or don't recognize that changes in your circumstances may mean there's less money to spend, resentment can build. Then, you'll have two problems to deal with: the original issue over your finances and the damage it's caused your relationship.

In their own words:

'When we returned from working overseas, our lifestyles changed dramatically. I accepted a salary that was far lower than what I'd been earning previously – and one that looked like it would never rise. I think Rob never accepted the adjustment and carried on spending like he used to.'

If one of you wants to give up work

If you decide to stop working because you want to be a full-time mum (or dad), it's normally expected that your other half will support you. But what happens if you want to stop work so you can retrain or do something completely different?

If you're unhappy in your current job, your plans for a change will probably be welcomed by your partner. No-one wants to see someone they love doing a job they don't enjoy or worse, one that actually makes them feel depressed. But they may be concerned about the financial implications for both of you, and you should be prepared to listen.

Your plans may mean your income will take quite a drop, or even disappear altogether, and your partner is bound to feel the financial pressure. They may feel that it's down to them whether or not the bills get paid and may even resent the fact that you've been able to pursue your dream while they can't.

> Work out exactly how much money you'll have coming in and how easy it will be to live on your reduced income. If you're the one who's planning to retrain, get as much information as you can about financial support, how long you'll have to study for and what the likelihood is that you'll get a job at the end of it. It's like drawing up a mini-business plan.

In their own words:

'My partner supported me when I was out of work, even though he was at the stage where he was building and developing his own career so he didn't have much in the way of disposable income. That was a real help.'

154

If one of you wants to start a business

Starting a business can also signal a massive change in lifestyle for both of you: the one with the business will probably be eating, living and breathing it, while the other may find they end up doing more of the chores, childcare or both.

It's also likely to affect how much you have coming in and the predictability of that income. Starting your own business requires real bravery on your part and you (and your partner) shouldn't underestimate that pressure. But you shouldn't let your enthusiasm for the idea mean that you lose touch with reality either. Often the expectations of people who want to start their own business aren't matched by what actually happens when they do.

In their own words:

'I went from being self-employed for several years to starting a company and have not yet emerged from the "feast and famine" cycle, which can be very hard. My partner is also self-employed which makes it more stressful if the "famine" hits both of us simultaneously and money's really tight.'

If you're spending too much

If you're spending too much, or you suspect your partner or spouse is, then honesty is the key. If you've run up the debts, you may feel guilty and embarrassed about what's happened, especially if your partner has been concerned about your spending in the past or has very different money habits to your own. You may think that they won't understand why you've ended up in debt. Well, the truth is that they may not. But ask yourself how you'd feel if the roles were reversed. Wouldn't you rather know the full picture at the time than when the debts became a real problem?

Debt counsellors say that they still see many people who come to them for debt advice owing many thousands of pounds that their partner doesn't know about. It doesn't just occur when couples have recently got together, where perhaps the trust is still building. In one case a woman who'd been married for 20 years had over £30,000 worth of debts which her husband was completely unaware of.

What debt counsellors also say is that when both partners are aware of the full picture, even if the debts were run up in one person's name, it's much easier to work out a repayment plan and it's generally much easier for the person who owes the money to stick to it.

Even if you keep your finances separate, it's useful to have someone to support you through the process. You're unlikely to tell your colleagues at work about your debt problem, you may not tell your family and you may not even confide in your friends. And if you don't tell your partner but suddenly start spending a lot less (because you've stopped spending the bank's or credit card company's money), they may wonder what's going on.

If you want to get some help on how to get back on track now, return to Chapter 4 and look at the advice on paying off debts. Pay off the most expensive loans or credit cards first and cut up your cards so you're not tempted to spend more. If you're worried about going overdrawn, ask your bank to take away your overdraft facility or opt for a basic bank account where it's impossible to go overdrawn.

Know where your money is going

It may be that your circumstances haven't changed a great deal, but you just seem to have less money than you used to. If that's the case, you've got to find out where the money's going – so now's the time to start a spending diary.

It may seem like a bit of a faff, but hopefully if you followed the advice in Chapter 4 you'll have realized just how valuable one can be. And there are several good software programs that will make the job much easier. Next write down where you think you can make cutbacks and then look at your spending diary again. Maybe there's something you missed first time round?

Then draw up a new budget using the template on page 53 and once you've completed it, give yourself a (free or low-cost) reward. It's important to acknowledge that by drawing up a budget and getting on top of your spending, you've done something that many people find too hard to deal with.

What if your partner won't join in?

I understand that facing up to the reality of your financial situation may not be easy and it will be harder if your partner doesn't want to face it at all. You can't make them join in, but there are steps you can take to make it easier:

- Draw up a list of what you'd like to talk about. It can really help you clarify what's important.

- Keep your conversation focused on financial matters. Don't make it about other issues in the relationship.

- Prioritize what you'd really like to change and work out a way forward in those areas. For example, ask them if they're happy if you don't use your credit card in the future, or if you cut back on meals out.

 Get a neutral professional involved. Suggest you go and see a debt counsellor or a financial adviser who can take an overview of your financial situation. It may be easier if someone else comes up with a plan that you can both follow.

In their own words:

'It's not been easy to talk about money ever. Ben knows how much I earn but he doesn't tell me anything. Money was supposed to be a joint decision, but if one holds back, you've got no way of making the decisions you want to make.'

Creating money

It may be that a little extra cash would make the difference between being able to adapt to your situation and getting into debt. One or both of you may be able to find ways of increasing your income. If your responsibilities at work have changed, or you've hit your sales targets consistently, you could ask for a pay rise.

If you can't create extra wealth this way, then you may be able to find some additional money by cutting your bills. Follow these steps and find out how much you could save.

 Switching supplier: Your utility, telephone and internet bills may well make up a larger part of your expenditure than you realize. You should check to see whether you can get a better deal on your gas, electricity, mobile and broadband deals and policies like car and household insurance.

158

Remortgaging: If you're on a standard variable rate deal, then you could probably cut your monthly mortgage payments by a significant amount if you switched to a tracker, fixed rate or discount deal. When I was writing this book, the standard rate at the Halifax bank was 7.75 per cent. But you could switch to a two-year tracker deal at 5.69 per cent, or a two-year fixed rate deal at 5.49 per cent with another lender.

If you have a £150,000 repayment mortgage you will save £213 a month (or over £2500 a year) by switching to the fixed rate deal and £195 a month (or over £2300 a year) with the tracker rate.

Credit cards: If you've allowed a balance to build up on your credit cards, switch to a 0 per cent deal and set up a standing order so that you pay off the debt by the time it runs out.

Savings: If you're paying into a savings account every month, you may want to consider diverting some of your money into paying off your debts. A lot of us feel reassured by having a cushion of money that we can fall back on, but it's better to get rid of debts that you're paying a high rate of interest on first.

If you need more detail about different price comparison web sites, refer back to Chapter 4.

CHAPTER 10

What happens if it all goes wrong

No-one gets married or moves in with their partner thinking their relationship will break up, but the sad fact is that many thousands of couples split up every year. Britain has one of the highest divorce rates in Europe: it's estimated that 40 per cent of marriages will end in divorce and among cohabiting couples the percentage of relationships that split up is higher.

Dealing with divorce or the breakdown of a relationship is one of the most stressful experiences that anyone can go through. The decision – which is often made by one partner – is just the beginning of an emotional rollercoaster.

I can't give you advice on how to deal with that emotional rollercoaster, but I can tell you what to expect from the legal process, what steps you can take to protect your own financial situation and how to ensure there is less room for surprises. And that may just mean you are able to feel a little more in control of at least one aspect of what you are going through.

Going through a divorce could mean you are faced with a legal process you never thought you'd have to get to grips with and have to make financial decisions at a time when emotions are running high. If you lived with your partner but weren't married, it may also be the first time you realize just how few legal rights you have.

Sadly, the breakdown of your relationship isn't the only devastating event you could face. Many thousands of people die unexpectedly and, for whatever reason, death (in common with money) remains a taboo subject in the UK. Not only will you have the overwhelming grief to deal with but you will have to tell everyone about your spouse's or partner's death, from close friends and family to a succession of companies you may never have spoken to before.

Divorce and breakup

Dealing with the shock

When you first split up, the emotional anguish will take over, but the financial consequences will also be preying on your mind. You may be worried that you'll have to move out of the family home, that your spouse or partner may have run up debts or that they won't pay the bills they're supposed to.

Whether you're married, in a civil partnership or living with your partner, you'll need to think about issues like who will stay and who will leave the home and what that will mean for both of you. How will you cope financially in the short term?

There are some basic first steps you need to take.

Step 1: Your children

Your children will be your primary concern. How will they be affected emotionally by the breakup and how much contact will they have with you and your partner in the future? These are serious issues, but are not really within the remit of this book. If you'd like advice, I'd suggest you look at the Directgov web site (www.direct.gov.uk) where there's a page on divorce and relationship breakdown. Alternatively you can look at Advicenow's leaflet called 'Parents Apart', which is on its web site.

> If you are living with your partner, you will only be able to get financial support for your *children* from the non-resident parent. You have no right to any maintenance or financial settlement of your own. But, as I explained in Chapter 3, that may change in the future.

However, your children's financial future will also be the priority during divorce proceedings or the breakdown of a relationship. Many divorcing parents worry about getting the Child Support Agency (CSA) involved because it has such a bad reputation for delayed and bungled payouts.

At the time of writing this book, the government has announced plans to replace the CSA with the Child Maintenance and Enforcement Commission (C-MEC) but it's not giving much detail about how the new agency may work.

What we know at this stage is that the C-MEC is supposed to:

- encourage parents to make their own child maintenance agreements

- simplify and streamline how child maintenance is calculated, so that money gets to parents (and therefore children) more quickly

- get tougher with parents who don't pay maintenance.

You don't have to get the CSA involved in working out how much maintenance should be paid, although it does arrange all cases where the parent with care receives income support or jobseeker's allowance.

If you're not on those benefits, you can reach a private arrangement (which doesn't have to involve a solicitor) or you can use the courts. A private arrangement means you're both in control of what happens and if you're still on reasonably good terms, it may help you to keep or even build on that relationship. It's also quicker and easier to set up than using the courts and doesn't have to cost anything.

The disadvantage is that it's not legally enforceable, so unless your partner or spouse wants to keep to the arrangement, you can't make them. However, you can turn a private arrangement into a legally binding one by using a 'consent order'.

> If you and your partner or spouse can't agree on how much child support should be paid, you will have to apply to the CSA. You cannot go to court to get a court order except to get a top-up to cover additional expenses like childcare costs and school fees.

Step 2: The house
If you own your home
When you're going through a divorce you may worry that your ex will try to sell the house from under your feet or perhaps that you will be left to pay the mortgage on your own.

Your home is far more than a financial investment; it's a place you've shared while you've been together. When it comes to how the house will be divided, that will be down to the courts if you are going through a divorce or dissolution of your civil partnership. If your live-in relationship has broken down, your rights are much more precarious.

If you own your house in joint names, it cannot be sold or remortgaged without your consent. If you are married and it's registered in your husband or wife's sole name, you can ask a solicitor to register 'matrimonial home rights', which will appear as a charge on the Land Registry and will protect your position.

At this stage you should try to make sure the status quo is maintained and that the mortgage and bills are paid. If you've got a joint mortgage you're each responsible for the entire mortgage, not just your 'half'. One party can't get their name taken off the mortgage agreement just because they've moved out. The lender would have to be satisfied that whoever is left can afford the mortgage.

> You might be able to take a 'payment break' or 'payment holiday' if finances are stretched. Interest is still added, but you don't have to make payments for several months.

As I outlined in Chapter 3, couples who live together and are not married don't have the same rights. If the house isn't in joint names, the best you can hope for is that you'll be entitled to a percentage of the proceeds.

In their own words:

'When I split up with my partner, we owned our flat jointly and had to get it valued. He made me an offer based on a valuation that was way too low, but didn't want me to get a second or third estate agent in. I ended up losing out financially, because I couldn't face the fight.'

If you rent

If you are married, it doesn't matter whether the rental agreement is in both names or just one, as you both have the right to live there (unless the court has ordered otherwise).

If you live together but the agreement is in your partner's name, you usually have no right to stay there if they ask you to leave. Many public sector landlords ask cohabiting couples to sign a joint tenancy, which gives you equal rights and responsibilities. If you decide to convert a joint tenancy to a sole one, you're both jointly responsible for the rent until a new tenancy agreement is drawn up.

If the agreement is in your partner's name but they want to move out, you may be able to get the landlord to transfer it to your name alone, but they're not obliged to do so.

Step 3: Joint bank accounts

If you have joint accounts you should talk to your partner or spouse about writing to the bank to close the accounts. You will both need to sign the letter. If you prefer, you can contact the bank and ask it not to allow payments with just one signature in future, or get it to take away any overdraft facility. If you do nothing and your ex goes on a spending spree then because it's a 'joint account' you each have responsibility for the full debt amount.

> Be aware that even though it's a joint account, some banks will deal only with the 'first named', i.e. the first name to appear on the agreement. So the second-named person could find the banks won't act on their instructions.

If getting both signatures on a transaction is not practical (if one of you has moved away, for example), an alternative would be for you to split whatever is in the joint account and open two new separate ones. You'll have to inform all the companies you have direct debits with and make sure they're happy with the new arrangement.

Whether you decide to open two separate accounts, or insist that both of you sign for transactions on your joint account, don't waste time in acting. Otherwise you could be faced with trying to negotiate with your ex to repay debts. It's always better to safeguard your position than to try to reclaim money after the event.

In their own words:

'It took me months to get my name taken off the joint bank account. I needed both our signatures and Mark, my ex-partner, was so antagonistic that he simply refused to do it. My only other option was to freeze the account, but I thought that would just make things worse.'

Step 4: Credit cards

You and your spouse or partner may each have a credit card with the same company and from the same agreement, but in the UK there's no such thing as a joint credit card. What's important is whose name is the first one on the agreement (the principal cardholder). Whoever that is has to pay the bills.

If you're the principal cardholder, you should contact your credit card company and tell them what's happened. The card company will probably ask you to destroy the second card, and will either let you carry on with the existing agreement or draw up a new one in your name only. Don't forget to cancel any direct debits or standing orders that your spouse or partner may have set up.

Step 5: Joint debts

Any debts or loans that are in both your names (whether that's with your spouse or your partner), you are both legally liable for. If you have joint debts, tell the lender that you have split up and that you don't want any changes to the account (i.e. the amount of the loan increased) without you being informed. Likewise if bills or arrears are in your name but your ex had agreed to pay them off, you should check what's actually happening.

Make sure the lenders have up-to-date contact details for you. If they want to take you to court for unpaid debts they don't have to ensure you've received correspondence, and a county court judgment will seriously damage your ability to borrow for the next six years, so try to avoid it at all costs.

> There's an odd quirk of law that means if you are married or in a civil partnership you are each responsible (jointly and severally liable, in the jargon) to make sure your council tax bill is paid. This means that if one partner normally pays the bill and they leave, or just fail to pay it, you are liable for the bill.

Getting expert advice

This section is going to concentrate on divorce, but it also applies to the dissolution of a civil partnership. If you're in a live-in relationship that's breaking down, it's probably useful for you to know about the different legal advice options, but the financial outcome of your split will be down to what you and your partner are able or prepared to sort out between you and possibly the complexities of property and trust law.

> You may feel that you want your ex to be financially punished if they've treated you badly, but behaviour is only rarely taken into account in divorce and dissolution and it won't affect the financial settlement.

The only exception is 'financial conduct', which means, for example, that if your spouse or civil partner has been having an affair and has spent a lot of money buying gifts for their lover, that might be taken into account. Financial recklessness, such as large gambling losses, might also be viewed as financial conduct.

If you're confident you understand what your rights are or you and your spouse or civil partner are able to sort out a financial settlement amicably, you'll probably need only the minimal involvement of a solicitor.

If that's not the case, finding out where you stand could be invaluable. It should give you some useful information and may reassure you that your worst financial fears won't be realized. Some solicitors will give one advice session free of charge or at a fixed cost, but you should make sure you find out how much it would cost to carry on using a particular solicitor.

If you and your spouse or civil partner are able to divide everything amicably between you, you should still get a solicitor to draw up a court order. If you don't, the financial claim remains 'open' and your ex could come back years later asking for more money.

Checklist of things to think about:

- Who will stay in the house and how will the mortgage or rent be paid, or will the house have to be sold?

- Bills such as council tax, gas and electricity may need to be put into the other person's name.

- Tell your mortgage lender and household insurer that you've split up. Your ex will probably have to sign a form to be taken off the household insurance, but it's more complicated with the mortgage.

- Don't ignore debts and joint accounts.

In their own words:

'Often money is the last thing that gets sorted when you split up, but in a way it should be the first, because – unless you split up amicably – you always think you can't push your ex to do something in case it makes them retaliate financially.'

Types of help available

Online divorce sites

There are quite a few sites on the internet offering to arrange your divorce. Prices start from around £65. Some offer email or telephone-based help and will fill in the forms for you, others won't. If your situation is straightforward (i.e. you've had a short marriage and there are no children), it may be worth considering, but if you have children to think about you're probably better off using mediation or a solicitor.

Advicenow has a downloadable guide to divorce available from www.advicenow.org.uk/divorce. If you're breaking up from your live-in partner there's also a 'breaking up checklist' to download.

Mediation

Mediation is a totally different approach from using a solicitor. Instead of each party having their own solicitor, there's one (or sometimes more than one) impartial mediator who's there to help the couple reach an agreement.

While the mediator can give you legal information, they won't give you tailored legal advice. The idea is that you can get the facts out in the open so that the mediator can try to move the discussion towards an agreement.

Some people say mediation is not a good idea if one person is much more dominant in the relationship, but others believe that it can be used in most divorce cases unless there's been domestic violence.

> If you have CLS funding (which is the latest name for the replacement for legal aid) you have to go for one meeting with a mediator. Some experts believe this is counter-productive as mediation works best when it's voluntary.

Mediation is generally cheaper than using the courts, but it's not necessarily cheaper than a simple legal process where both parties have already agreed who gets what.

> ### Finding a mediator
>
> Try the UK College of Family Mediators (www.ukcfm. co.uk), The Family Mediators' Association (www.fmassoc. co.uk) or National Family Mediation (www.nfm.org.uk).

Solicitors

Collaborative law: Using a solicitor does not have to mean a confrontational approach. Something that's relatively new, but becoming more popular, is 'collaborative law', which is a cross between mediation and traditional legal advice.

Each party has their own solicitor, and both the couple and the solicitors sign an agreement saying they'll do the best for the whole family. The idea is that you have a series of round-table meetings with your spouse and your solicitors and both of you know exactly what's being discussed.

Importantly, the solicitors also sign an agreement saying they won't go to court, which increases their commitment to reaching an agreement this way. If the process does break down, you'll have to hire new solicitors. You can find a collaborative family solicitor through their web site, www.collabfamilylaw.org.uk.

Traditional legal advice: Here the solicitor will find out about your own situation and advise you on what your rights are. They will communicate directly with your spouse or civil partner (or their solicitor if one has been instructed) and keep you informed about any agreements that are being negotiated. You'll often have at least one face-to-face meeting, but after that your solicitor may keep you informed by letter, email or telephone, although you will have to see them again if you go to court.

A lot of us feel intimidated by the legal language and in some cases by the formal settings of a solicitor's office, but a good solicitor will understand the emotional state you may be in, although it's not their job to be your counsellor. For a start, their fees are much higher than a counsellor's.

If you want counselling advice, Relate is an obvious place to start (www.relate.org.uk). You can get advice in person, by phone or by email. It will cost around £30 for a tailored email reply and £45 for a 60-minute telephone advice session. Some law firms also have counsellors or therapists attached to their practices.

You should be able to tell the solicitor everything that you feel is relevant to the divorce or dissolution, but you should also realize that the more money you spend on legal advice, the less there is to divide between the two of you. So, to get the most from your appointments (which means you'll also keep the costs down) try this:

- Get hold of bills and financial papers relating to you and your spouse's financial situation before you go to the meeting. Summarize them into a simple schedule of income, assets, pensions, liabilities and outgoings.

- Write down a list of questions you would like answered.

- Make notes when you are at the meeting, or bring a friend or relative who can do that for you.

- Look for information on the internet (but be careful about the credibility of sites you're not familiar with).

- Resist the temptation to use your solicitor as an emotional prop.

- Don't make unnecessary phone calls or send unnecessary emails. Calls and emails are not free and are normally charged in six-minute blocks.

A solicitor will set out their costs in the 'terms of engagement' letter. Make sure you take the time to read it and are happy that you understand how you're being charged for advice.

Finding a solicitor

If you know someone who's been through a divorce ask them for a recommendation. Otherwise try the Resolution web site (www.resolution.org.uk). Resolution is the new(ish) name for the Solicitors Family Law Association, a group of solicitors who sign up to a code of conduct which means they try to deal with divorce cases amicably. In Scotland you should try the Scottish Family Law Association web site (www.fla-scotland.co.uk).

Costs of divorce

Solicitors' fees will be the most expensive part of the divorce process. Fees vary between different parts of the country but you're usually looking at upwards of £150 an hour for a partner's services and far more in London.

There are other costs as well: a fee to file the divorce petition, to swear an affidavit and to apply for a decree absolute at court. If your divorce is straightforward, court and other costs could add up to £350 plus your solicitor's fees.

Help with divorce costs

If you can't afford a solicitor, you may get help through the CLS (Community Legal Service) funding scheme, which used to be known as legal aid. However, there are strict limits on how much you can earn before you qualify for help and the calculation as to whether you'd qualify for CLS help or not (and if so, how much) is, unfortunately, fiendishly complicated and not something I can easily simplify.

You can get further information from the CLS web site (www.clsdirect.org.uk). It includes a calculator to help you work out what you might get. Bear in mind that if you do get help with legal costs you'll have to pay it back from any money or assets (such as the house) that you receive.

Hidden assets

Don't be tempted to hide your financial assets. Many divorcing couples assume that the richer partner is squirrelling money away so it's out of reach of the courts. A private detective once told me that when someone comes to see him about whether their husband or wife has hidden money or property, they are correct in around 90 per cent of cases. However, sometimes a lot of money can be spent on forensic accountants or private detectives, which may not be justified by the value of the assets they uncover.

If you suspect something's being hidden, don't be tempted to go on a 'fishing expedition' just for the sake of it. While the courts take a dim view of anyone hiding assets they are equally unimpressed if you've used dodgy or illegal methods to get the information.

Divorce in Scotland

The divorce process in Scotland is very different to that in the rest of the UK. The main differences are that there is no minimum period before you can get divorced; you can't get divorced until the financial issues have been resolved; and Scottish courts divide up only what the couple had when they separated (rather than at the point of divorce).

In Scotland it's also rare for support to be paid after divorce. Whereas in the rest of the UK the courts have a fair amount of discretion over who gets what, in Scotland there are basic principles that govern the way property and other assets are divided.

In simple terms, there's a presumption that property acquired during the marriage (excluding gifts or inheritance, and up to the point of separation) is divided equally, no matter whose it was in the first place.

Civil partnerships

Because the Civil Partnerships Act was passed relatively recently, the breakup of civil partnerships (or dissolution, to give it the correct legal term) is relatively uncharted water. But in broad terms, financial settlements take into account the same factors as divorce.

The death of your spouse or partner

Divorce is devastating, but losing the person you love is likely to mean the grief will be overwhelming. No death is easy to deal with, but it may be worse if your loved one dies at a young age or unexpectedly. If you haven't lost someone close to you, you really can't understand what this kind of loss feels like.

If you aren't getting enough support from your friends and family, I'd suggest you contact a counselling service or an organization like Cruse Bereavement Care (www. crusebereavementcare.org.uk). The government's web site Directgov (www.direct.gov.uk) has a section called 'end of life'. Don't be put off by the title as it has lots of useful information.

There are no quick fixes that will help you and no shortcuts to speed up the grieving process. It will be harder if you have to sort out a financial tangle because your partner or spouse hasn't left a will or wasn't particularly organized about their financial affairs.

In their own words:

'It's really scary when the bank freezes all your partner's accounts and the bills start piling in and you have no money, but try not to panic. Get a friend to help you work out what you have and what you need to pay. And don't spend money until you have it. It sounds obvious but what might look like a straightforward life insurance policy is never guaranteed until it is in your bank account.'

First days

Here are some key steps to take in the earliest days:

- You will need to register the death within the first five days. If you're not married to your partner, you can only do this in limited circumstances.

- If you're the executor of the will, you will need to apply for probate (officially you apply for a grant of probate), so that the money and assets can be distributed. You can do this yourself or ask a solicitor to do it for you.

If you use a solicitor, find out exactly how much they are going to charge you. Some charge a 'value' element: it's basically a percentage of the value of the estate added onto their hourly rate. This can add up to tens of thousands of pounds.

- If there's no will, you have to apply for 'grant of letters of administration' if you are married. Unmarried partners do not have the right to do this.

You will also have to tell organizations such as the tax office and the DVLA, and companies such as bank, mortgage lender, building societies, credit card companies, etc. that your loved one has died.

Be aware that while some companies are very good at handling calls from bereaved partners, others are pretty shocking. You may find you are passed from pillar to post and that you have to send in duplicate copies of death certificates.

If you're married or in a civil partnership, you may be able to claim a bereavement allowance or a bereavement payment, depending on your circumstances. Your spouse or civil partner has to have paid a certain level of National Insurance contributions or be able to meet other conditions (relating to how they died). Cohabiting partners are not entitled to this benefit.

> You'll need lots of legally certified copies of the death certificate as many companies will want one before they will close the account or remove your spouse or partner's name, so get at least five or six copies. Some insurers will only change household policies into sole name once they've seen the death certificate and even firms like mobile phone companies ask for them.

If you are getting divorced or have been bereaved, don't make long-term decisions in the first few months. If you have inherited some money or received it from a financial settlement, put it in a high-interest rate savings account while you think about what you need to do. Make only essential financial decisions as things will be hard enough anyway. Once you've managed to survive the first few months, you should be able to see what you really want or need to do a little more clearly.

CHAPTER 11

Growing wealthier together

This book is designed to help you and your partner take control of your money and the decisions you make, but I don't want you to feel that once you stop being a slave to your overdraft or debts, you become ruled by your 'money management timetable'. But the truth is that sorting out your money isn't a one-off. To get the best from it and to become wealthier, you need to keep an eye on your finances and be prepared to shake them up from time to time.

You may have made some decisions that were absolutely right at the time, but may not fit in with your current plans, and your financial habits may need a bit of a spring clean. Even if you think you're on top of your spending, you could be wasting money without realizing it. For example, you might have insurance policies that duplicate cover, you could have signed up to gym membership with the best of intentions or you may be paying more than you need for essentials.

Spring clean

A spring clean, de-clutter, financial detox, cash diet. However you prefer to think of it, it's designed to do the same thing – to get rid of any waste and help you keep the pounds, not lose them.

I think the psychology of these exercises is really important so, as in Chapter 4, it's a good idea to start where you know you can make savings and move onto the areas that need a bit more discipline later on.

Go through your bank statements and look at all your regular payments to see whether there's any duplication. These days insurance policies often have extras, some of which are free and some of which you're offered for a few pounds. You may be paying for mobile phone insurance when it's already covered by your 'all risks' contents policy.

> If you can save £50 a month, that adds up to £600 a year. Invest that in a cash ISA earning 5.75 per cent and after 10 years you'd have £8083 and after 20 years, £22,429.

If you haven't checked that you're getting a good deal on utilities and your mobile phone in the past 12 months or so, make time to do so. Paying by direct debit is great for getting a discount, not so good for making you aware of what the service is costing. That's why companies push it so strongly.

You may be spending money on things you don't really use. OK, so gym membership may be a bit of a clichéd example, but that's because so many people sign up to an expensive one and don't use it. Pump iron or cancel your membership.

Look out for money that slips through your fingers. If you're taking out money from the cash machine, only to go back a couple of days later for more, it may be time to add up what you're spending on coffees, magazines, DVDs, etc. Allow yourself some treats, but cut down.

> If you can save another £30 a month and you invest it in your pension, after 20 years you could have an extra £800–£1000 a year in income when you retire.

Financial review

This isn't the same as a financial detox. Instead the idea is that you make a list of all the financial deals you've signed up to – such as your mortgage, life insurance or income protection – and your investments – such as ISAs or your pension – and make sure that the choices you made at the time still fit in with your plans.

It's also a good way of making sure that the deals are still competitive and that your investments are on track to deliver the returns they are supposed to.

You can sort out your bank account yourself – and possibly your mortgage as well – but for the rest I would suggest you get the help of a professional such as an independent financial adviser. It's particularly important with long-term investment plans where you may not be able to tell if they are performing well or not.

Bank accounts

Look at your bank current and savings accounts. Switching current accounts can be a hassle, but it can also make good financial sense (but be careful if you are planning to apply for a mortgage – see Chapter 5). While you're comparing banks, have a quick look at your savings accounts.

Set a date in your diary for a financial detox and review. You don't have to plan it months in advance; it's whatever suits you. But make sure that you check all your finances every year; more frequently for those that need it. January is a good time because that's when you'll be feeling the financial pinch and so your mind will be more focused on getting the best from the money you have and trying not to spend cash that isn't yours.

Mortgage

Reviewing your mortgage isn't just about getting the lowest rate. As your needs change, you may find you want to switch to a different type of mortgage. You may want to remortgage to an offset or flexible deal, so you can pay off your loan as quickly as possible.

Life insurance

At the moment the life insurance market is very competitive, so prices are falling. If you took out life insurance more than five years ago, it's definitely worth looking to see if you can get a better price.

Investments

Investments are meant for the long term, but that doesn't mean you should ignore them for years. Many of us make decisions without thinking of how they fit in with investment plans we've already got and policies we've already taken out.

There are several reasons for reviewing what you have:

1. **You may have too much money in one type of investment which means you're taking on more risk than you realize. Perhaps you've piled money into an equity ISA with the same company, or even the same fund, every year.**

2. Even if your money was carefully split between shares, bonds and cash when you invested it, so that you reduced the risk, one asset (such as shares) may have done better than others. This means your carefully balanced investments are now out of kilter, which means they will need 'rebalancing'.

> Rebalancing simply means selling off some of those investments that have risen sharply and buying more of others that have remained stable. It may sound counter-intuitive. Why would you want to get rid of investments that have done well? Well, there are two reasons. First, you don't know for how long they'll carry on doing well and second, the whole idea of investing is to buy when prices are low and sell when they're high.

3. If your fund is being managed by professionals (rather than just tracking a stock market index like the FTSE 100 or FTSE All-Share), the top-performing manager who was in charge when you took it out may have left. Their replacement may not be as good.

4. It gives you a chance to consolidate your investments. Over the years, you may have accumulated many different accounts and policies. If the numbers start to get out of hand, think about streamlining what you have.

5. There may be changes to the law which you don't know about, or if you do, you may not realize their implications. It could mean you miss out on tax-efficient opportunities or investments.

6. **New products and funds are being launched all the time and some developments and innovations are worth knowing about.**

Pensions

If you're paying into an occupational pension scheme, you won't necessarily have much choice about where your money is invested. If it's a final salary pension, you won't have any say about where the main part of your pension is invested, but you can choose where to invest if you decide to pay extra into your scheme.

With money purchase and group personal pensions you *can* choose where your money is invested, while with stakeholder pensions you can switch or transfer to different funds with no penalty.

More importantly, your review will help you work out whether you're on track for your retirement. If you want a rough idea, you could use one of the pension calculator sites on the internet. There's one on www.pensioncalculator.org.uk, which is operated by the Financial Services Authority and the Association of British Insurers.

If you're in an occupational scheme and you don't have the information to hand, contact the scheme trustees or your human resources department to find out whether you can increase your contributions and how to go about it.

Review your will

You don't need to review your will every year, but it is something you should do if your circumstances change or if the Chancellor makes some significant changes to tax thresholds or laws. In 2007, he made it easier for married couples or those in civil partnerships to transfer their IHT allowance, while a few years ago he tightened up the rules on trusts.

Your house or investments may have risen in value so that your estate might face the prospect of an IHT bill, in which case you should see what steps you can take to reduce your liability. What you do and to what extent you want to minimize any IHT bill is down to you, but it's definitely worth looking at the options available.

The road to financial bliss

If you've followed the advice in this book, you should be well on the road to financial bliss. Here are a few last thoughts to keep you there:

- Don't give yourself a hard time if you make a bad decision or if your budgeting plans go wrong. Guilt is likely to stop you from doing something positive about it. Face up to what's happened, tell your partner, get advice if necessary and work out a plan that will get you where you really want to be.

- Understand that sometimes your partner will make decisions about money that you won't like. But it works the other way as well. The ideal is not necessarily to have the same approach to money, but for each to feel comfortable with the decisions the other makes.

- Allow yourselves to dream, especially if it means you feel more determined to make your dreams a reality.

- Realize that money can't buy you happiness, but being in control of it will give you both more choice about how you live your life together.